DUBLIN'S ARCHITECTURAL DEVELOPMENT
1800-1925

CONTENTS

EUROPEAN YEAR OF THE ENVIRONMENT

With the generous sponsorship of the Irish Permanent Building Society, DUBLIN's ARCHITECTURAL DEVELOPMENT is published in the first quarter of 1988 as a special contribution to the European Year of the Environment and in celebration of the Dublin Millennium. In accord with the objectives of the European Year of the Environment, it is hoped that this survey of an important period in the architectural development of the capital will increase understanding and awareness of our environmental heritage. In the year when Dublin celebrates one thousand years of development it is fitting that attention should be directed to the built environment of the city and that due consideration be given to ways in which it can be enhanced.

DUBLIN MILLENNIUM
988~1988

FOREWORD

For convenience the history of European architecture is often divided into periods or styles. In Irish buildings of the period under review in this book the styles which principally affected their development were, firstly, the Renaissance style based on the classical architecture of Greece and Rome and secondly, the Medieval styles of Romanesque and Gothic which flourished throughout Europe during the Middle Ages. The former shaped the design and form of our Eighteenth Century and Early Nineteenth Century buildings, while the Gothic revival of the second half of the century was inspired by and based on earlier Gothic styles, principally English and French. Irish Medieval work only had a marginal effect. Style as applied to buildings may, therefore, be defined as a distinctive type of architecture distinguished by special characteristics of ornament or construction.

This book focuses attention on architecture of the period from 1800 to 1925. While much has been published on what are generally referred to as Dublin's Georgian buildings, the architecture which followed them has received comparatively little attention. The aim of this publication is to improve the balance in treatment of the city's architectural heritage. Nearly all the buildings mentioned are still in use and can be seen by citizens as well as by visitors to the capital.

Although architecture of the period 1800–1925 has been selected for special attention the limits are not rigidly applied. In dealing with the subject of architectural development some flexibility is necessary. Significant buildings erected prior to 1800, but which have been subsequently restored, altered and/or put to new use in the 1800–1925 period are included. Mention is also made of some alterations carried out after 1925 to buildings constructed between 1800 and 1925. The term architectural development is used in a broad sense, covering not only buildings of various types from the simple to the sophisticated but also other features of the cityscape including thoroughfares, bridges and street furniture, monuments and parks, all of which form part of the physical environment. Many well known buildings are included in the survey but so also are some lesser known ones and the County is covered as well as the City of Dublin.

Nearly all the photographs illustrating the book were taken specially for the purpose so that the buildings can be seen in their present context. The buildings may be readily identified from the exterior views shown but the importance of interiors must be emphasised. In illustrating books about Dublin publishers, with a few notable exceptions, have relied to a great extent on old pictures from the Lawrence and other well known photographic collections, reproductions of familiar period prints and drawings from old books and magazines. In the case of this book it was decided to use, as far as possible, hitherto unpublished photographs and so give readers a new look at a large number of Dublin's buildings as they now appear. There are only a few flashbacks of buildings which have since been substantially altered or demolished.

ACKNOWLEDGEMENTS

The authors wish to thank most sincerely the Irish Permanent Building Society for its sponsorship of *DUBLIN'S ARCHITECTURAL DEVELOPMENT 1800-1925* which enables TULCAMAC to publish this profusely illustrated book at a very reasonable price. In thanking the Society the authors gratefully acknowledge the kind assistance given by Mr. Enda Hogan, Executive Director–Marketing, and Mr. William A. Maguire, Director, Irish Permanent Building Society, in making the necessary arrangements.

The authors thank Mr. Ken Mawhinney, Director, *Environment Awareness Bureau*, for his interest and for expressing his approval of the project as an appropriate contribution to the European Year of the Environment. They also thank the Dublin Millennium Committee for its words of encouragement.

The generous practical assistance given by Mr. Joe Buckley, Managing Director, Corporate Graphics, is gratefully acknowledged. He was responsible for giving very helpful impetus to the project in its early stages. It was also a great advantage to have the manuscripts promptly and accurately typed by Anna Brioscú, Monessa Payne and Sheena Bourke.

The book was expeditiously and satisfactorily printed by the Leinster Leader. For this we thank all the staff involved. We are especially grateful to Mr. Michael Kane for his courtesy and efficiency.

The publishers thank the National Museum for permission to reproduce the cover illustration from the drawing in its possession and to thank Ms. Felicity Devlin, Education Officer, for arranging this. The picture by T. Raffles Brown, which shows Sir Thomas Deane's design for the National Library and the National Museum was reproduced in *The Irish Builder* in March 1893 and was shown at the International Exhibition in Chicago.

The authors thank all those who provided information about buildings mentioned in the book.

It would not have been possible for the authors to undertake this project without the willing co-operation of their wives. The authors, therefore, wish to put on record their grateful thanks to Peggy McDermott and Anna Brioscú for facilitating them and supporting them in carrying out the work.

THE CLASSICAL TRADITION

The beginning of the 19th century saw the passing of the Irish Parliament, when the Act of Union between Great Britain and Ireland came into force in January 1801. The centre of Irish affairs changed from Dublin to London. As a result many of the Irish nobles, their ambitions unrealised, sold up their city houses and moved to London, or else retired to their country estates. While this change was taking place Dublin was still a comparatively new city, mainly Georgian in character, with few relics of its historic past. At the same time conditions of life and trade were changing. The legislative reforms of the thirties led to the growth of middle class influence which was the hallmark of the century, while the Factory Acts slowly improved the lot of the working classes. Few great town houses were built. The buildings were, apart from churches, mainly for new purposes and often in styles different from those that went before.

These changes in architectural style or fashion go back to the closing decades of the 18th Century when Palladianism in building declined and the neo-classical style began to develop. Palladianism had its origins in the work and writing of the Italian architect, Andrea Palladio (1518-80), whose style of Renaissance architecture became popular in Britain and Ireland and dominated much of the work of the 18th century. Like Palladianism the neo-classical style was based on Roman work, but the elements were used in a different way. In Dublin the facades of Aldborough House and those of the Chapel and Examination Hall of Trinity College, designed by Sir William Chambers, illustrate neo-classical forms. The porticos, like those at Trinity, no longer project boldly beyond their facades but are almost part of the wall surface, while the proportions and arrangement of the windows suggest a remote or reticent appearance, which is one of the marks of the neo-classical manner. Neo-classical art was not, however, generally accepted in this country; its apparent austerity did not appeal to the Irish taste.

Later in the 18th century a further change in building design occurred. This phase, known as the "Greek Revival", came here from England and was influenced by the monuments of classical Greece. It became an important and widespread movement in this country, in which the elements of Greek rather than Roman architecture — columns, mouldings, decoration, etc. — were used, often with great skill and effect. It was adopted not only for churches such as St Mary's Pro-Cathedral (1815), Marlborough Street, and St Stephen's, Mount Street, but also for public and domestic work, such as the General Post Office, O'Connell Street, with its fine portico of Greek Ionic columns. Another example, Nelson Pillar (erected 1808, destroyed 1966) was once Dublin's most massive street monument and one of the finest columns of its kind in Europe since the age of Trajan.

Although Irish architects of the late 18th and early 19th centuries were, on the whole, faithful followers of classical art, the first steps towards popularising medieval

LIMESTONE HEAD BY
EDWARD SMYTH & SON,
EAST DOORWAY,
CHURCH OF THE MOST
HOLY TRINITY,
DUBLIN CASTLE.

The Chapel Royal, Dublin Castle, was designed by Francis Johnston and built in 1807-14. It was renovated in 1943 and was consecrated as the Catholic Church of the Most Holy Trinity. It has some fine oak carving and fine decorative plasterwork. Elaborate fan-vaulting is a special feature.

The Record Tower was refaced with calp as part of the renovation work carried out under the direction of Francis Johnston, architect, in the early Nineteenth Century.

CHURCH AND
RECORD TOWER,
DUBLIN CASTLE.

architecture were taken in the 18th century. This manner of building was seen as a romantic alternative to the neo-classical style. It was used mainly for domestic work and country churches. The former were generally castellated mansions based on the English Tudor style; the latter were of a rather jejune type of Gothic, more economical to build than classical work. By 1828 a number of churches were built in this manner, including those in Booterstown, Chapelizod, Swords and Donnybrook, while in the city the north transept of St Patrick's Cathedral was rebuilt. The new chapel of St Mary's, later to be called "The Black Church", was designed in the Gothic style by John Semple. These were churches of the Establishment, as few Catholic churches had been built by that time.

The first native architect of note to attempt a more scholarly approach to Gothic architecture was Francis Johnston (1760-1829). While not a master of Gothic detail he had a good knowledge of Gothic design, as may be seen in the Castle Chapel (1807-14), now the Church of the Holy Trinity in Dublin Castle, as well as the entrance of the Royal Hospital, Kilmainham, the archway of which was moved from its original position on the Quays. Johnston's great reputation as an architect does not, however, rest on his medieval or his institutional buildings, prisons, asylums and the like, but rather on his mastery of classical design. Although not a Dubliner (he was born in Armagh) he gave Dublin some of its outstanding Renaissance buildings, such as St George's Church, Hardwicke Street; the General Post Office; Nelson Pillar and, not least, he was responsible for the alterations to the Parliament House carried out for the Bank of Ireland with a dramatic sense of architectural composition comparable with Soane's Bank of England, treated to mask a number of internal courts and halls. These buildings formed the greatest contribution to civic pride since James Gandon's Custom House and Four Courts.

The railway stations form another important group of 19th century classical buildings, all worthy additions to the capital. They were sited at some distance from the city centre to avoid traffic congestion and to reduce noise and smoke in the area. They served the old Great Southern and Western Line, the Great Northern, formerly the Dublin and Drogheda Railway, and the Dublin, Dún Laoghaire and Wexford routes, the respective terminii being the Kingsbridge (now Heuston) Station; the Broadstone; Amiens Street (now Connolly) Station; Westland Row (now Pearse Station) and Harcourt Street Station (now offices). They were all designed with exceptional ability and varied in treatment from the massive Broadstone (c.1841 and now closed) by J S Mulvany, to the gay, almost palazzo-like facade of Kingsbridge (1845-46) by Sancton Wood. The last of the city terminii was Harcourt Street, designed by George Wilkinson about 1859.

As few cities can point to such a fine series of railway buildings, their architects deserve some notice. Wilkinson came to this country from England in 1839 as architect to the Poor Law Commissioners of Ireland, to build the workhouses, buildings which for long caused feelings of popular revulsion on account of their unhappy associations, and the inhuman treatment meted out to their inmates. In all about 160 were built, mostly on a standard plan, to accommodate eight hundred

ST. FRANCIS XAVIER'S CHURCH, UPR. GARDINER STREET.

St. Francis Xavier's Church, Upper Gardiner Street, was designed by John Keane of Mabbot Street, for the Society of Jesus and built in 1829-32. A special feature of the nave is the coffered ceiling. The tall Greek Ionic portico is a striking feature of the exterior which blends with the streetscape.

The Chapel of St. Ignatius was built in the middle of the Nineteenth Century.

The Jesuit school was moved into Belvedere House in 1832 and extensive additions were later made to what became known as Belvedere College.

The building of the Franciscan Church of the Immaculate Conception, Merchants' Quay, designed by Patrick Byrne, was commended in 1830. The original design has been greatly altered. External features include a large cupola and a belfry in the form of a miniature Greek temple.

The Neo-Classical interior has two orders of pilasters, the lower is Doric and the upper is Corinthian.

ADAM AND EVE'S, MERCHANTS' QUAY.

to one thousand paupers. The basis of planning was the segregation of the sexes so that families were split up regardless of age or condition. Although larger than their English counterparts, the standards of construction and finish were lower. Wilkinson tried his best to blend these buildings into the Irish countryside, but their size and harshness made his task an impossible one. On his professional travels throughout Ireland Wilkinson became interested in Irish quarries and in the remains of old Irish buildings, publishing in 1845 "The Practical Geology and Ancient Architecture of Ireland", one of the earliest Irish treatises of its kind.

Towards the end of the 19th century the workhouse system gradually changed to meet the demands for better treatment of the poor, taking on some of the character of hospitals. But the system, as such, lasted to 1921, when the workhouses were finally abolished. The South Dublin Union (facetiously referred to as No. 1 James Street) formed the nucleus of St Kevin's, now St James's Hospital, which, if plans are fully realised, will rise phoenix-like to be one of the largest and best equipped in the country. Wilkinson's skill as an architect is not reflected in the workhouses, but may be gauged from his handling of Harcourt Street Station, with its elegantly proportioned archway and brickwork in keeping with its late Georgian surroundings.

John Skipton Mulvany (1813-70) was a son of T J Mulvany, the artist, keeper of the Royal Hibernian Academy, and biographer of James Gandon. He was apprenticed to William Deane Butler, the architect of Connolly Station, the earliest (1844-46), but architecturally the least interesting, of the series. Mulvany's treatment of the Broadstone was more original, and designed with an almost Egyptian-like massiveness. He may have been influenced by P C Hardwick's work at the old Euston Station, London. Mulvany also designed the railway station and the Royal Irish Yacht Club at Dun Laoghaire, as well as the fine colonnaded shelter to one side of the Broadstone. His mastery of classical architecture cannot be doubted, the treatment of which was sometimes tinged with a native originality which made him the last of the great Irish architects of the century.

Sancton Wood (1816-86) was English. Articled to the notable Sir Robert Smirke, his practice consisted mainly of railway work. He built stations in England as well as in Ireland, where he acted as architect to the old Great Southern and Western Railway.

Between the Union and the Famine the most important event was Catholic Emancipation, 1829. This gave many new hope and confidence in the future. Although Catholic churches had been built in the city prior to 1829, a magnificent series of new churches, chiefly in the classical style, was built within the following ten or fifteen years:

    Adam and Eve's, 1830, by Patrick Byrne
    St Nicholas of Myra, Francis Street, 1832, by John Leeson
    St Francis Xavier, Gardiner Street, 1832, by J. Keane
    St Paul's, Arran Quay, 1835-7, by Patrick Byrne

PRESBYTERIAN CHURCH, ADELAIDE ROAD.

Another church on Adelaide Road, the Catholic Apostolic Church, designed by E. T. Owen, was built in the 1860s.

The Presbyterian Church, Adelaide Road, built in 1840, closes the vista at the end of Earlsfort Terrace but due to its dark colour it does not have a strong visual effect, even though the portico stands on a high podium.

The Wesleyan Centenary Church on the south side of St. Stephen's Green was designed by Isaac Farrell and built in 1843. It is now part of a bank premises. By coincidence, Isaac Farrell also designed the Dublin Savings Bank (now the Trustee Savings Bank) in Abbey Street, built in 1839.

The former Methodist Centenary Church, St. Stephen's Green, has a granite facade and Port- land stone columns.

The Wesleyan congregation, which formerly attended the Methodist Church, St. Stephen's Green South, now share Christ Church, Leeson Park, with the Church of Ireland parish.

FORMER METHODIST CHURCH, ST. STEPHEN'S GREEN.

St Andrew's, Westland Row, 1837, by James Boulger
St Audoen's, High Street, 1841-6, by Patrick Byrne

Although these churches are inferior in design to St George's, and their 18th century predecessors, they form a vital link in the classical traditions of Dublin, and bridge the gap between work of the 18th century and the coming of the Gothic Revival. They are mainly exercises in the treatment of facades. The front was usually composed of a portico of classical columns surmounted by a cupola or small bell tower finished at the top with a dome. These churches viewed from the front, or as seen from a distance, form dignified compositions carefully proportioned and effectively detailed. The interiors, however, are of comparatively little interest, with the exception of St Audoen's and St Andrew's Westland Row. St. Stephen's, Mount Street, affectionately known as the "Pepper Canister" in reference to its cupola and dome, was a little earlier than its Catholic counterparts, and Bowden's design may have influenced their treatment. St Audoen's, on the other hand, has a more original structure. As seen from Cook Street, it rises fortress-like from its sloping site, so that the sides and back have a more dramatic impact than the front, the portico of which was added at the end of the century, long after the death of Patrick Byrne, its architect. Byrne was born in Dublin about 1783. Catholic Emancipation gave this local architect a unique opportunity. In the years between that event and his death in 1864 he designed up to a dozen of the Dublin diocesan churches, mainly, but not all, in the Renaissance style. The most ornate of these is the Church of Our Lady of Refuge (1850-56), Rathmines, in the design of which, so Italian in character, he may have been influenced by a Roman cleric, a Father Gentili, who came as a missioner to Dublin, where he died from typhus in 1848. The church, with its great central dome, was gutted by fire about 1920. The interior was restored on the same general plan, cruciform in shape, with the dome dominating the skyline. This reconstruction was by the firm of Dublin architects, W H Byrne and Son. Patrick Byrne also tried his hand at Gothic architecture, but with less success. Gothic churches are mainly in the suburbs, such as the Church of the Visitation, Fairview, and the Old Church at Raheny.

Besides the Catholic churches of the post Emancipation period, the classical style was also used for churches of other denominations such as the Presbyterian Church (1840), Adelaide Road; the Church of St Matthias (1842), Hatch Street (since destroyed); St Stephen's, Mount Street; Trinity Church, Lower Gardiner Street (now the Labour Exchange), built of brick and stone dressings and once one of the largest in the city. The most massive of all was the Methodist Centenary Church, St Stephen's Green, by Isaac Farrell (c.1843). Only the facade with its great Ionic portico and steps, remain, as the interior was destroyed by fire. Farrell's exclusive use of hard Irish granite instead of the traditional granite walling and Portland stone columns was an interesting, but unsuccessful departure, as the stone failed to mellow in the Dublin atmosphere. Farrell also designed the Trustee Savings Bank (formerly the Penny Bank), Lower Abbey Street, in the same material and in a similar neo-Grecian style (1839).

CHURCH OF IRELAND, MONKSTOWN.

The Church of Ireland in Monkstown, built in 1830, is an unusual Gothic design by John Semple, who also designed St. Mary's Chapel of Ease, St. Mary's Place (The Black Church), built about the same time. Other Protestant churches designed by John Semple include those at Donnybrook, Kilternan, Rathmines, Whitechurch, Rathfarnham and Tallaght.

Adjacent to Semple's church in Monkstown is St. Patrick's Catholic Church (1864), designed by Ashlin and Pugin. This building with its tall spire contrasts with Semple's composition featuring towers and turrets.

Longford Terrace, Monkstown, built in the third quarter of the Nineteenth Century, was designed as an architectural unit.

Unusual
entrance
doorway.

CHURCH,
MONKSTOWN.

THE GOTHIC REVIVAL I

Churches

When Johnston died in 1829, Augustus Welby Pugin, who became the chief apostle of the Gothic Revival, was still in his teens. Although Gothic had been practised in the 18th century, little earnest work was accomplished in either England or Ireland before Pugin's day. The Irish Gothic Revival, which began in a tentative way at Slane Castle, became, in time, the vehicle of an extraordinary architectural expression based on the widening of scholarship and a growing interest in the medieval period. These pursuits, combined with a sincere belief in its appropriateness as an architectural style, underlay the revival, which reached this country from England towards the middle of the century. Its greatest exponent was the English architect, Augustus Welby Pugin (1815-52) whose work, and particularly his writings, wielded the widest influence. Pugin maintained that architectural style had a moral basis and was not a matter of personal choice. He advocated Gothic architecture, as opposed to classical, because he regarded the former as Christian in its origin and use. In particular, he recommended the type known as Early English as its purest form. This phase originally flourished in England about the 13th century.

Between the time of the Romantic movement which brought into fashion the castellated manions of Johnston, the Morrisons, Nash and others, and the rising tide of the Gothic Revival, the Famine intervened. All types of building, except those for relief work, slowed down. After the Famine the reconstruction of the physical fabric of the Catholic church in Ireland began in earnest. This great undertaking, financed mainly by the contributions of the faithful, spread the use of Gothic architecture throughout the land, as convents, churches and schools were built in great numbers. After Pugin's death his influence waned and Gothic became more elaborate, but not necessarily better. In this country the trend was to follow English examples, but Irish work was, on the whole, not as progressive as in Britain. The "rustic" style of design with low rubble walls, large roofs, few buttresses and simple openings as used in England for country churches, was not employed here. Few churches of any size or standing were built of brick. Stone was the traditional building material. The use of "structural polchromy" (the use of materials of different colours as part of the structure of the building), popularised in England by Butterfield and others, had only limited application in Irish church work, but was more freely used in secular buildings.

After Pugin's death, religious associations linking Gothic with Catholicism gradually declined. Gothic was widely and generally adopted by the Church of Ireland. While

NICHOLAS
STREET,
PATRICK
STREET
AND ST.
PATRICK'S
CATHEDRAL.

The Iveagh Trust was responsible for the building of flats and other facilities in Patrick Street at the beginning of the Nineteenth Century.

SS. Augustine and John's Church, Thomas Street, designed in the Gothic style by Edward Welby Pugin and George C. Ashlin was begun in 1862, opened in 1874 and completed in 1911. Ruskin described this Church as a poem in stone but unfortunately the red sandstone has not weathered very well. The tower, which rises to a height of almost 50m, has a peal of bells. It was designed by William Hague and the statues of the Apostles were carved by Pádraig Pearse's father. The stained-glass windows by Mayer of Munich are a special feature of the interior.

SPIRE,
SS. AUGUSTINE
AND JOHN'S CHURCH,
THOMAS STEET.

the buildings of the latter remained faithful to English precedents, a growing knowledge of French Gothic (popularised by the writings of the French architects and historians, Viollet-le-Duc, Corroyer and others) led to the use of this form — partly as something novel and partly as a stylistic distinction separating the buildings of Catholicism from those of the reformed churches. SS Augustine and John's (c.1860), Thomas Street, designed by Pugin's son, Edward Welby, with his Irish partner, George C Ashlin, represents a high mark in the use of French Gothic. Lastly, the Gothic style was selected by the Presbyterian and Methodist churches, thus giving a dominant style of building which finally extinguished the classical traditions of the 18th and early 19th centuries.

In the planning of churches, Pugin's dictum that a church should be more than a "preaching box" was not always adopted. In his view the church should have, at least, two distinct parts or units, nave and chancel, clearly defined both inside and out. This was often ignored in favour of a shallow sanctuary cut off from the nave or body of the church. In Protestant churches the main difficulty in re-introducing chancels was to find a use for them. They were mainly used by the choir which, in Catholic churches, was generally in a gallery at the back of the nave, while the sanctuary, or chancel, was reserved for the altar.

Generally speaking, two types of church plans were used. First, a simple rectangular shape dictated partly by the size of the church and partly by reasons of economy. This consisted of a nave, with or without transepts (arms at right angles to the nave) so that the interior was one large open space uninterrupted by columns or pillars; thus every member of the congregation had a clear view of altar and pulpit. The main effect depended on proportions and scale and the relation of the sanctuary or chancel to the nave. The sanctuary was usually richly treated but often cramped and mean in dimensions. The interiors, sometimes of large spans, were finished either with an open timber roof or sealed in with vaulting. In the former, the usual type of truss used to carry the roof timbers was known as the "hammer beam". This had no origin in Irish work, as far as is known, but was taken directly from English examples where the open timber roofs used in medieval times form one of the minor glories of Gothic architecture. As used in Irish work the timbers employed were usually too thin and although sufficient in strength, they often look weak and improverished. Further, the rich colours of medieval decoration were omitted, so that the decorative effect of the roof was lost. Where vaulting was used it usually was of plaster on a lathed backing.

For more elaborate churches a different plan was adopted. This consisted of a central nave separated by columns or piers from side passages or aisles, sometimes with transepts and chancel. This layout gave a more interesting inteior composed of contrasting spaces, glimpsed rather than seen through the perspective of arches and piers, leading the eye towards the altar. These new Gothic Revival churches with their buttresses, pointed arched windows and soaring lines of towers and spires contrasted vividly with the classical ecamples, particularly in this country where so little medieval architecture survived. Some of these churches, while impressive externally,

ST. MATTHEW'S CHURCH, IRISHTOWN.

St. Matthew's Church of Ireland, Irishtown, was built in 1703 for the mariners who used the port of Ringsend. It was rebuilt under the direction of J. F. Fuller, architect, in 1878, retaining the original tower.

Several other churches were built in the Sandymount district in the middle of the Nineteenth Century, including the Anglican St. John's (1850); the Catholic St. Mary's, Star of the Sea; the Methodist Church on the Green (1864) and the Presbyterian Church (1870).

The Sisters of Mercy moved into Lakelands in 1870.

St. Bartholomew's Church, Clyde Road, Ballsbridge, designed by Thomas Henry Wyatt of London, was opened in 1867. The spire was never built but there is an interesting octagonal tower over the choir. This features decorative pinnacles and a miniature Irish round tower at the north-east corner. The church has a nave, aspidal chancel and transepts. The headquarters of the Knights of Malta are now accommodated in the former rectory.

ST. BARTHOLOMEW'S CHURCH, CLYDE ROAD.

often have an internal effect of remoteness, while the lifelessness of the enrichment and the mechanical nature of the carvings carried out in soft imported stone (for ease of working) often appear inappropriate and out of place in our surroundings. On the other hand, one of the most pleasing aspects of the Gothic Revival was that of excellent construction based on traditional materials and methods which have stood the test of time. Even in the dullest conditions the native stonework rarely appears too grey or dismal. Unfortunately, Irish marbles were rarely used. Altars, pulpits, rails, memorials, etc. were usually carved in Italian marbles. The type known as "statuary", which was commonly used, was of a cold white colour, which is still depressing and chilly in appearance as time has failed to soften the effect.

A large amount of early Gothic work in Ireland was carried out by English architects. Among the most able and active of these were the Pugins, father and son; William Butterfield (1814-1900); R C Carpenter (1812-55); W Burges (1828-81); George Goldie (1829-87) and Thomas Henry Wyatt (1807-80), whose work in the Dublin area includes St Bartholomew's Church, Clyde Road (1865), Sandford Church and St John's, Sandymount, the latter jocosely known as the "Devil's Church", a reference to the gargoyles adorning the facade. The interior of St Bartholomew's surpasses in decoration other city churches, particularly in the colourful treatment of the open timber roof and chancel.

Most of the Irish work of the elder Pugin lies outside Dublin, but in the city area he designed the chapel of the Loreto Abbey, Rathfarnham. George Goldie (Goldie, Child and Goldie) was one of the most active in Ireland of the English architects of the period. He designed, among other works, St Peter's (1860 approximately), Phibsboro, often regarded as his best work in Ireland. The apse, side chapels, transept and crossing are by Goldie, but the nave was completed later by the local architects, Ashlin and Coleman. A tower at the crossing built to Goldie's design was demolished as it was considered to be unsafe. William Butterfield, one of the most distinguished of the English architects, was responsible for the chapel at St Columba's College (c.1850) Rathfarnham. R C Carpenter was principally associated with the restoration of St Patrick's Cathedral, Dublin, following repairs by Pack.

After Pugin's death, his son, Edward Welby Pugin (1834-75) established his own practice, which included secular work as well as Catholic churches and monasteries. His buildings, although generally more ornate and ambitious in their scope, rarely attain the quality of those of his distinguished father. In this country his name is associated with George C Ashlin. Ashlin was born in County Cork about 1840. He was a pupil, and later a partner of Pugin in designing churches in Cork, Cobh, Wexford and Dublin. In the capital, Catholic churches at Monkstown (1864) and Donnybrook (1863) as well as the massive SS Augustine and John's (1862-95 approx.), Thomas Street, are typical of their work. The latter tower, however, was completed later by the Dublin architect, William Hague, and is the highest in the city. After the dissolution of the partnership in 1870 Ashlin practised on his own account continuing to build in a rather ornate manner as in St Kevin's (1870), Harrington Street, and also in the Parish Church of All Saints at Raheny, Co. Dublin, which he designed for Lord

MERRION HALL,
LOWER MERRION STREET.

Merrion Hall, Lower Merrion Street, designed by Alfred G. Jones was built in 1863. A non-denominational church, it can accommodate a very large congregation.

Close to Merrion Hall, the large red brick building on the corner of Fenian Street and Westmoreland Row incorporates Oriel House, which now provides additional accommodation for the Dental Hospital (designed by Caulfield Orpen), another red brick building, in Lincoln Place.

The Congregational Chapel, 13 Lower Abbey Street, a tall red brick building, which has survived the large-scale redevelopment in the area, was acquired by the Salvation Army in 1910.

UPPER PART OF FACADE,
MERRION HALL.

Ardilaun about 1885. The firm later became known as Ashlin and Coleman when Thomas A Coleman entered into partnership with Ashlin at the beginning of the 20th century.

Andrew Heiton of Perth, who had Irish connections, designed Protestant churches in Dun Laoghaire and Rathgar. He is perhaps best known for the elaborate treatment of Findlater's (Presbyterian) church built about 1864 on a commanding site in Parnell Square. These churches, with many others, emphasise the domination of Gothic architecture as the accepted church style of the second half of the century. A rare example of a classical building of ecclesiastical character erected at this time was Merrion Hall, Lower Merrion Street, completed in 1863 under the direction of Alfred G Jones who later emigrated to Australia where he died in 1915. His chief works in Dublin were the International Exhibition Buildings (1865) in Earlsfort Terrace, the main structure of which was designed as a permanent centre for concerts and exhibitions.

During the sixties Irish architects gradually took over from English practitioners. Of the native architects one of the most prominent was J J McCarthy (1817-82), who built extensively throughout Ireland, mainly in the Gothic style. He was primarily a church architect with a good knowledge and belief in Gothic architecture, but he tended to be coarse in detail and sometimes over elaborate in design. His Dublin buildings include St Saviour's (1859), Dominick Street (with later additions by Ashlin); Mount Argus, Harold's Cross; the Capuchin Church, Church Street; and the chapel at All Hallows College, Drumcondra. McCarthy's last and most impressive work was the chapel at Maynooth College, which he took over from Pugin, but the College in its original form was completed by William Hague.

GRADUATES' MEMORIAL BUILDING, TRINITY COLLEGE.

CHAPEL,
ST. COLUMBA'S COLLEGE,
RATHFARNHAM.

The chapel at St. Columba's College, Rathfarnham, designed by William Butterfield, was dedicated to St. Mark in 1880. A simple building in the Early English Gothic style, it is based on a plain rectangular plan. The belltower over the main entrance is the dominant external feature. The interior is divided into nave and chancel. The walls of the nave are lined with sandstone and those of the chancel are finished with coloured tiles.

St. Columba's College, founded in 1842, was originally located in County Meath. In 1849 it moved to Rathfarnham. The College was built in the grounds of Hollypark, formerly the residence of Jeffrey Foot, which was converted into the Warden's House.

CHAPEL,
ST. COLUMBA'S COLLEGE,
RATHFARNHAM.

THE GOTHIC REVIVAL II

Collegiate Chapels

It may be of interest at this stage to see how three outstanding architects, two English and one Irish, interpreted the Gothic style to suit a particular design, that of a college chapel, and to compare the results.

The earliest of these was Augustus Welby Pugin's design (1839) for the chapel at the Loreto Abbey, Rathfarnham, a convent boarding school outside Dublin. The chapel is enclosed within a surrounding corridor or cloister. Based on a cruciform plan the main feature of the interior is a high octagonal lantern, rising like a tower over the crossing of nave and transepts. Springing from the corners of the crossing the lantern has no intermediate supports to interrupt the sanctuary, over which it floats like a canopy or baldachino. As one approaches the altar the soaring lines and proportions carry the eye upwards until it rests on a glazed attic or clerestorey. The lantern, recalling that at Ely Cathedral, England, is three storeys high built in receeding stages, the first and second with traceried lights are related to bedroom corridors over. This enables sick or inform nuns to hear Mass at these windows. The top storey, rising over the adjoining roofs is glazed. This gives a downward light illuminating the altar which is directly below as well as the decorative paintings covering the interior surface of the lantern.

Apart from the sanctuary and its lighting the chapel is generally simple. The plan is based on a Greek cross, one with equal arms. The nuns' chapel is in the nave. The transepts or side arms are reserved for the pupils. The fourth arm at the back of the altar is hidden by a reredos or ornamental screen and acts as a retro-chapel. The main lines of the chapel and its details (caps, mouldings, tracery, etc) are based on the decorated phase of English Gothic (14th Century). In contrast the sanctuary and its treatment, which was in its day almost unique in Ireland, strikes a dramatic note and remains a lasting tribute to the genious of its architect.

The second chapel is at St Columba's College, a boys' school also in Rathfarnham. It was built in the 1850s, more than a decade after the Loreto Chapel, and was the work of William Butterfield (1814-1900), a notable English architect and follower of Pugin. In this instance the chapel is freestanding and completely detached from the college proper. Planned as a rectangular building and designed in a simple rural style, based on the Early English Gothic of the 13th century, it is less elaborate than Pugin's work. Its simplicity is, indeed, an integral part of its beauty.

Externally the main feature is the bell tower, the lower part of which acts as the entrance. The tower is placed towards one end of the chapel, and is related to, but not connected with a college entrance. Internally the chapel is divided into nave and chancel. The nave has collegiate oak seating, above which the walls are lined with sandstone. The chancel walls are treated with coloured tiles arranged to give a pannelled pattern, a remarkably restrained effect for an architect who was so fond

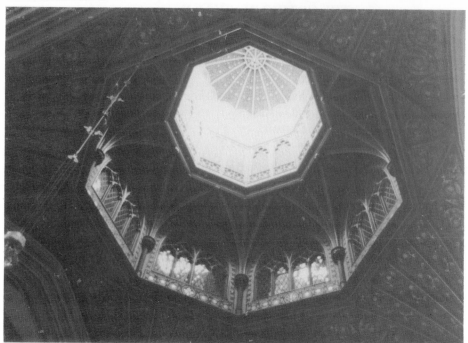

LANTERN LIGHT,
COLLEGIATE
CHAPEL,
LORETO ABBEY,
RATHFARNHAM.

The high octagonal lantern light over the crossing of the nave and transepts is three storeys high, the first has traceried lights to rooms and corridors, the top one is a glazed clerestorey.

The Chapel at Loreto Abbey, Rathfarnham, designed by Augustus Welby Pugin, was built in 1839. It is cruciform in plan and is surrounded by its own corridor or cloister. The nuns' chapel is in the nave, the transepts are reserved for the pupils.

INTERIOR,
COLLEGIATE
CHAPEL,
LORETO ABBEY,
RATHFARNHAM.

of colour. Spacially the chancel is not a separate unit, but a continuation of the nave, differentiated from the latter mainly by the wall treatment. The ceiling of timber sheeting has simple arched beams carried on brackets or corbels related to the external buttresses.   Inside,   the general effect is one of repose heightened by the rather sombre lighting; also by the simplicity of treatment and the general absence of ornament, which is confined mainly to the organ gallery off the nave and to the sedilia or seats for clergy in the chancel wall. The dramatic effect of the Loreto chapel is not to be found here.

The third chapel, at All Hallows College, Drumcondra, was originally designed about 1860 by the Irish architect, J J McCarthy, but following a fire in 1895 it was rebuilt in its present form by George Ashlin. As part of a seminary, the plan takes into account the space required for ordination ceremonies as well as the provision of side altars for individual Masses. The layout consists of an aisle-less nave with collegiate seating or stalls ending in a large semi-octagonal chancel. Opening off the chancel are side chapels, which give the building a cruciform shape.

Internally the treatment is more ornate than either the Loreto or St Columba's. The walls are divided into bays by attached columns with large traceried windows between, and with rose windows at the gable ends. Generally well-proportioned, the interior has the added dignity of height, while in the design effective use is made of the spacious sanctuary and of a polygonal timber ceiling, but the plastered and painted walls (now covered with large pictures) lack the dignity of stone. Externally the design is of less interest than the interior; the main front looks a little pretentious, but the side elevations are simpler and happier in scale. A curious feature of the exterior is the elaborate iron cresting which runs along the ridge of the roof.

Although All Hallows Chapel is a dignified and functional building, it misses some of the spirit of Gothic art which animates the design of the other two. The spirit becomes apparent again in the work of William Henry Lynn (1828-1915). Lynn was one of the most talented architects of the period. Born in Co Wexford, he was a pupil and later partner of Sir Charles Lanyon of Belfast. Lynn was remarkably successful in competition work, securing first place for Chester Town Hall; the Houses of Parliament, Sydney, New South Wales; Chateau of St Louis (1875), Ottawa, Canada; government offices; extensions to Queen's University, Belfast; Barrow-in-Furness Town Hall, etc. In Dublin he designed St Andrew's Church, Suffolk Street, which he won in competition (1862). In the competition another entry by Lanyon and Lynn was placed second and that of Raffles Brown third. Others who competed included Deane & Woodward (fourth), Thomas Turner (fifth) and Rawson Carroll, an   Irish architect (sixth). An example of Carroll's ornate style is Christ Church and Asylum, Leeson Park, Dublin. St Andrew's is, perhaps, the best example of the work of the Gothic Revival in Dublin. Although not a large church, it follows the basilican plan of nave, aisles and chancel. Internally it is simple, well-proportioned and restful. Built in the early English style, it forms a dignified composition externally, particularly effective when the fine broach spire and arcade are seen in perspective along Church Lane. In St Andrew's an unusual touch in Irish urban churches is the use of

PRESBYTERIAN CHURCH
AT THE JUNCTION OF
HIGHFIELD ROAD AND
RATHGAR ROAD.

Christ Church, Rathgar, was opened in 1859.

The first stone of the Methodist Church, Brighton Road, Rathgar, was laid in 1874. It was designed by Thomas Holbrook.

The Church of Ireland, Zion Road, Rathgar, designed by Thomas Welland, was built in 1862. Externally the walls are faced with granite, calp and limestone and internally there are Caen stone columns.

ZION PARISH CHURCH
AT THE JUNCTION OF
ZION ROAD AND
BUSHY PARK, RATHGAR.

polygonal rubble blocks of multi-sided stone fitted together to give a rustic effect. The Unitarian Church (1862), St Stephen's Green West, was also Lynn's work. It is a good and original example of a church on a narrow street frontage. It is now flanked by modern office buildings. Lynn was a versatile architect and also an able designer in the classical style.

Another prominent church architect of the day was Joseph Welland (1798-1860). He was apprenticed to Bowden, the architect of St Stephen's, Mount Street, but fortook the classical manner of his master in favour of the reigning Gothic style. First appointed as an architect to the Board of First Fruits and to the Ecclesiastical Commissioners (1833) he became their sole architect ten years later. His output was enormous, building or altering churches throughout the country. In the Dublin area his work includes Zion Parish Church, Rathgar; St James's, Inchicore and St John's, Clontarf. St. John's was built in 1863 to designs by Welland and his partner, Gillespie. Cruciform in plan, Early English in treatment, it is typical of the style adopted by the Ecclesiastical Commissioners. The main feature of the church is the fine tower and spire placed assymetrically to form a porched entrance to the nave. The chancel was added later.

These churches, like so many others, reflect little of the progress of the 19th century. Architects were mainly concerned with problems of style and so missed the technical advances of the day. Francis Johnston was quick to realise how cast iron could be adopted for window tracery, but this process, as used in the Castle chapel, was anathema to the pure Gothic generation. It was, therefore, left to the engineers to exploit the advantages and to make use of the new materials (principally glass, iron and later, concrete) in a variety of structures, such as bridges, viaducts, sheds, station roofs, etc. But these, according to the architects of the time, were not architecture and, therefore, *moral* values or questions of style did not arise. Furthermore, some architects were of the opinion that only by the faithful study of the past could a contemporary type of architecture be created, overlooking, perhaps, the influence of materials and structure on design. This may have been among the principal reasons why no great or lasting monument of the Gothic Revival was built in Dublin. In other fields of planning, apart from churches, where precedents were not so strong and where contemporary opinion was favourable, worthwhile advances were achieved as in the design of exhibition halls, hospitals, libraries, etc.

The most important ecclestiastical work of the Gothic Revival in Dublin was, therefore, not the new work but the restoration of the cathedrals of Christ Church and St Patrick's. Christ Church was restored by the English architect, George Street (1824-81). Street had a great knowledge of Gothic architecture and, as Christ Church was in the English medieval style, Street let himself go. Backed by the wealth of Henry Roe, the Dublin distiller, he practically rebuilt the church (1871-8), but in a way which is today regarded as somewhat drastic. For instance, he changed the appearance of the tower, giving it a new papapet, high angle turrets and new windows for the belfry. The synod hall he linked to the church by a high bridge. Nevertheless, Street's work is very good and full of interest.

ST. PATRICK'S
CATHEDRAL.

St. Patrick's Cathedral dates back to the early Thirteenth Century but it has undergone many changes since then. The spire was built in 1750 to the design of George Semple. The Lady Chapel, designed by the English architect, R. C. Carpenter, was built in the first half of the Nineteenth Century. Restoration work, financed by Sir Benjamin Lee Guinness, was continued by Sir Thomas Drew.

At the beginning of the Twentieth Century slums were cleared from the north side of the cathedral and a park laid out.

ENTRANCE DOORWAY,
ST. PATRICK'S CATHEDRAL,

St Patrick's was not altered to such an extent. The early work of restoration was carried out by R C Carpenter, an English architect and an able Gothic designer. He was mainly responsible for the restoration of the Lady Chapel (c.1864), but following a disagreement with Sir Benjamin Lee Guinness, who was providing the funds, he retired from the work. Sir Benjamin acted for a time as his own architect, with less happy results. Further restorations were carried out by Lords Iveagh and Ardilaun. Sir Thomas Drew acted as their architect and made safe the nave, the present vaulting of which is not of stone but of modern lath and plaster construction. Sir Thomas Drew (1838-1910) was one of the outstanding architects of his day. He was born in Belfast, and after an apprenticeship to Sir Charles Lanyon, he practised for a short time in the North before moving to Dublin in 1862, where he built up a large and varied practice. In the Dublin area an example of his church style is the Presbyterian Church at Howth Road, Clontarf, built of rough grey granite walling, with red sandstone quoins and dressings. This polychromatic treatment gives the church an individuality which is particularly effective in the high tower with its corner pinnacles. This type of treatment, unusual in Dublin, recalls in its proportions and outlines, English work of the 13th century. Drew was also responsible for St Kevin's (C. of I.), South Circular Road, and also for the restoration of Marsh's Library, while the last remaining relic of the medieval fortifications and gateways of the city, St Audoen's Arch, was also restored and repaired, with new battlements and parapets by Sir Thomas, about 1880.

Apart from churches of the Gothic Revival, some others may be mentioned. The new front for St Ann's, Dawson Street, by Sir Thomas N Deane (c.1868) is a good example of Romanesque design to suit a street frontage. Around the corner in Molesworth Street were the associated parish buildings, the Parochial (Molesworth) hall and St Ann's schools. Both were examples of the successful adaptation of brick to Gothic design used effectively with high pitched roofs and dormer windows. The school, built about 1857, was an early and charming example of the use of Gothic for secular purposes. Both were destroyed in 1978.

University Church, St Stephen's Green also uses coloured and modelled brick in the facade or entrance porch. This church (1856) was designed by J Hungerford Pollen for Cardinal Newman, then Rector of the Catholic University of Ireland. It is unique in Dublin, on account of its Byzantine manner. The rich and exotic interior is a fine example of the use of marble wall linings and applied colour. Although there are carved ornaments, these are subservient to the general effect. The treatment of the apse, the altar and its furnishings deserves study. A third church of interest is outside the city, but in the Dublin region, St Doulough's, near Malahide, Co. Dublin, which was restored and enlarged about 1863. The original church, dating from medieval times, directed the architect, W H Lynn, towards a study of the native Irish style as a possible alternative to English or French Gothic for church design. His work helped to bring about a short-lived revival of the Hiberno-Romanesque style which originally flourished in this country during the 12th and early 13th centuries. The small church at Lusk, Co. Dublin, by J J Robinson, is an example of a 20th century adaptation of this treatment.

ST. DOULOUGH'S CHURCH, BALGRIFFIN.

The old stone-vaulted church, St. Doulough's,* Malahide, dates back to the Thirteenth Century. Various alterations and additions were carried out in later times. The tower and stepped battlements are thought to have been built in the Fifteenth Century. A Gothic Revival addition was made in 1863-65. Funds for the Nineteenth-Century Church were collected by a commitee chaired by Lord Talbot de Malahide. The architect, W. H. Lynn, designed the new building to harmonise with the old one. It was consecrated by Archbishop Trench in 1865. The Church consists of a nave, chancel and porch. The walls are of limestone in random courses and there are lancet windows.

*There are various spellings of this name (e.g. Doulagh).

St. Sylvester's Church, Malahide, was built in 1937. The spire, designed by George Ashlin, was added in 1901.

The Catholic Church of St. Michan, designed by O'Brien and O'Gorman, was opened in 1816. It was enlarged and the new front by George C. Ashlin erected in 1893.

The original Church of St. Michan, Church Street, was dedicated in 1095 and was reconstructed in 1685. The medieval tower is 37 m high.

A number of those who fought in the 1798 rising are buried in the churchyard.

ST. MICHAN'S CHURCH, CHURCH STREET.

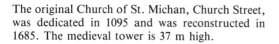

By the eighties most of the needs of the suburban parishes for new churches had been met and little new church work was attempted, except for rebuilding or extending existing buildings. This continued until the city began to expand after the First World War. By this time Gothic architecture had been phased out, but associated styles, such as simple Romanesque or Classical designs, were still used and acceptable. Gothic, which had started in the early 19th century as a romantic movement, became the great Christian style of the 19th century before it became the universal style under the leadership of Ruskin and his followers.

Aughrim Street Parish was constituted from St. Paul's, Arran Quay, in 1893. The Church of the Holy Family, designed by J. S. Butler, was opened in 1876. It was reconstructed by Doolin, Butler and Donnelly, architects.

At the time the church was being built fine houses had recently been erected on both sides of the North Circular Road as far as the Phoenix Park. Nearly all these houses can still be seen.

Other churches are illustrated on pages 204-243.

CHURCH OF THE
HOLY FAMILY,
AUGHRIM STREET.

DOUBLE
FRONTED
TERRACE
HOUSE,
UPPER
LEESON
STREET.

A variety of different house types was built in Leeson Street. The tall houses close to the footpaths in Lower Leeson Street contrast with some smaller houses in Upper Leeson Street which have only two storeys above basement and which have spacious front gardens. Changes in use, however, and opening up of gardens for car parking has changed the character of parts of the street.

A number of the original houses in Upper Leeson Street have been replaced by new buildings with pastiche facades.

TERRACE
HOUSES,
UPPER
LEESON
STREET.

THE GOTHIC REVIVAL III

Houses and Mansions

During the first decades of the century the city continued slowly to expand. Fitzwilliam Square and the adjoining streets — Baggot Street Upper and parts of Lower Leeson Street — belong to this period, and were mainly occupied by the rising professional and merchant classes of the city.

The shopkeeper of the day lived, as a rule, over his shop, but improved transport facilities encouraged many of the better off to move to new suburban or seaside villas. These suburban houses included many on the outer roads and squares of the period, such as Waterloo Road, Leinster Road, Wellington Road, etc. These houses continued the Georgian style, but with certain modifications, such as the use of painted fronts, the raising of the basement, and with details such as doorways based on the style of the Greek Revival. They generally reached high standards of design and of serenity that few can achieve today. At the same time, many people were living at a precarious level of existence, as Dublin experienced few of the benefits or, for that matter, few of the disadvantages of the Industrial Revolution. After the Famine, many of the Georgian houses, particularly those on the north side of the city, were turned into tenements, as a starving peasantry fled from the countryside. At this time Dublin was growing, but only slowly compared with the rapid expansion of Belfast. Only by counting in the outlying suburbs or villages such as Rathmines, Pembroke, Clontarf, etc., which were incorporated as townships about 1847, could Dublin numerically exceed that city.

In the sixties, renewed confidence in the future and a general increase in wealth, led to fresn building developments. Houses and villas, detached and semi-detached, cottage residences and terraces in various designs and style were built on existing, as well as on the new roads of the period. In 1861 Temple Road, Rathmines, was in progress, while Ailesbury Road was opened up and ready for building about 1865. Architectural style had changed. The influence of the Gothic Revival with bits of sham medieval work and unsympathetic brickwork were making an appearance, but the houses had still a dignity which is probably more apparent today than when they were built.

Houses for tradesmen and small merchants were usually of the cottage type, compactly built in terraces, such as may still be seen in some of the inner suburbs as, for instance, along the streets adjoining the South Circular Road. At that time these smaller houses had no w.c. or water supply; an outside privy and street fountain sufficed. In better class houses taps were usually at ground floor level and perhaps on the first floor, where there was also a w.c. As a rule there was no bathroom until later in the century. The hip bath, ewer and basin, were in common use for ablutions. Few large city houses date from this period. A good example of a fine Victorian town house is No. 52 Leeson Street.

COTTAGES, BALLSBRIDGE

The Pembroke Estate ensured that residential accommodation of a high standard was provided, making effective use of slate, brick and stone.

Wellington Road and Pembroke Road were developed in the middle of the Nineteenth Century, followed by Elgin Road, Clyde Road and St. Mary's Road.

TERRACED HOUSES, LEESON STREET.

Some of the more affluent merchants and gentry built new houses, or rebuilt old ones, on the outskirts of the city, sometimes in a pseudo-medieval or Romantic manner. The Morrisons, Sir Richard (1767-1849) and his son, William Vitruvius (1794-1838), were, with Francis Johnston, the leading architects of their day. Like the latter, they also designed in the Gothic style, although neither professed to be Gothic architects. The 12th century Castle of Clontarf was restored and extended (1837) by the Morrisons in the Tudor style, to form a picturesque composition of towers and bays carried out with rich and interesting details. A feature of the interior was the hall with gallery and staircase, but the full effect of these have been lost in later alterations.

A little further out, Sir Benjamin Lee Guinness built his country house, St Anne's, designed about 1860 by J F Fuller in a heavy Italianate style, which was a fashionable alternative to Gothic. This house (now destroyed) had, externally, no great architectural merit. It was, however, set in parklands of great beauty, planted and embellished with groves of trees, grottos, lake and ruins. This layout was continued by Sir Benjamin's elder son and successor, Albert Edward, later Lord Ardilaun. Although somewhat mutilated, St Anne's serves today as a public park. The garden and farm buildings which still survive indicate the splendid craftsmanship and materials of the Victorian period. These must be praised for their durability and effect, even if the latter appears to be somewhat strident. A local curiosity which illustrated the social distinctions of the day, was the tunnel under part of the grounds overlooked by the house. This, with its sunken approaches, screened from view the locals who used it as part of a right-of-way leading from Raheny to Clontarf. The sunken pathway was still negotiable up to the middle twenties, when it fell into decay and disuse.

Sir Benjamin Lee Guinness also built Iveagh House (now the Department of Foreign Affairs), St Stephen's Green, incorporating and extending adjoining Georgian houses behind a rather grandiose Portland stone facade.

In the sixties and seventies, public opinion favoured improvements in working class housing. These came about, however, only slowly. The mass of the population was crowded into reeking tenements, where the death rate from disease and deprivation was alarming. Due to overcrowding and lack of hygiene, epidemics and outbreaks of fever were common. The pioneeer work of the Dublin Artisans Dwellings Co. and of the Iveagh Trust (founded 1890) deserves recognition. The former provided cottages and small houses at modest rents, while the latter was engaged in slum clearance and in the building of houses and flats. The Bull Alley Scheme (1901-4) in the Liberties, is typical of these early measures by the Trust. Among the earliest (1894) were the Bride Street Estate, Blocks A to E, the work of Robert J Stirling, a Dublin architect.

Transport companies also provided housing for their workers in proximity to their places of employment. Tramway Cottages at Donnybrook and Clontarf are examples. Cottages were also built for some other groups of workers in the city and suburbs.

LOOKING OUT FROM CITY HALL

Thomas Cooley designed the Royal Exchange, Cork Hill, for the Dublin merchants and it was built on a fine site adjacent to Dublin Castle in 1769-79. The architect was appointed as a result of a competition in which James Gandon came second. In 1814 the stone ballustrade was built in front of the main entrance. Dublin Corporation bought the building in 1852 and had interior alterations carried out under the direction of Hugh Byrne, architect. Further alterations were carried out in 1867.

The Wide Streets Commissioners, who were in office from 1757 to 1840 were responsible for the planning of Parliament Street which was opened up in 1762. This was one of the first projects undertaken by the Commissioners who had such an important role in the development of the city.

Lord Edward Street, which runs from the City Hall to Christ Church, was opened in 1886.

PARLIAMENT STREET FROM THE CITY HALL.

The Dublin Corporation, with limited resources, also tried to alleviate housing conditions by the building of small blocks of flats or tenements. The apartments were grouped around a central staircase, which was constructed of stone with open galleries at the half landings. This functional design permitted the free circulation of light and air, and allowed for the sluicing of the steps and the ventilation of the staircase — a modest advance in hygiene compared with the timber stairs of the Georgian tenements and open hall doors of which encouraged dirt and abuse.

TERRACE OF HOUSES, CARNEW STREET, OFF COWPER STREET.

In the Eighteenth and Nineteenth Centuries brick was commonly used for facing large town houses but brick was also used for facing more modest dwellings. In Carnew Street a multi-coloured decorative effect was achieved.

MASONIC HALL, MOLESWORTH STREET

The Masonic Hall, Molesworth Street, was built in 1866. The building on the extreme left carries the date 1755 on the pediment.

Hewett's Corner is located at the junction of D'Olier Street and Hawkins' Street. A prominent feature of the decorative stone and brick exterior are the elaborate chimney stacks.

HEWETT'S CORNER, D'OLIER STREET AND HAWKINS' STREET.

THE GOTHIC REVIVAL IV

Other Secular Works

During the first half of the 19th century shops and business premises were not much different in scale or appearance from the houses of the 18th and early 19th centuries. Both were built mainly of brick with small-paned windows, the shops sometimes bow-fronted in the Georgian manner. There were no office buildings as such until later in the century. Economic expansion and new ideas gradually created a need for more buildings specially suited to office and commercial requirements. A good example of a 19th century office block in red brick is at Connolly Railway terminus, designed by Lanyon and Lynn of Belfast about 1879.

Following the Famine the quarter century from about 1850 was one of comparative prosperity. This increase in wealth was reflected in the size and treatment of the buildings, some of which are still promient features of the city streets. At first classical architecture prevailed as in the work of Johnston and that of his partner and successor, William Murray. The extensions to the College of Surgeons, St Stephen's Green, designed by the latter (1829) is a good example of late classical work.

However, the rising tide of medievalism in architecture, based on English influences, gradually eroded the old Dublin Renaissance style, which declined in quality and spirit until it finally passed away about 1860. Typical of this decline is the facade of the College of Physicians (1862), Kildare Street, designed by William George Murray, a son of William Murray mentioned earlier. This design was selected as the result of a competition. It may have been the most suitable submitted, but the external treatment is over-elaborate in relation to its scale. The present facade is a replica of the original, as the old stonework decayed beyond repair. Another classical building of almost the same date is the Masonic Hall, Molesworth Street, also built as the result of a competition (1866). This was won by the English architect, Edward Holmes of Birmingham. Holmes design reflects again a typical late Renaissance style rather foreign to Dublin, and one in which the simplicity of earlier work is lost. Most of the secular buildings of the mid-century onwards were, therefore, not of classical design but in the medieval manner. Some, like those of Deane and Woodward, compare more than favourably with the churches of the period, and can claim a place among the notable buildings of their day.

The Deanes were a family of Irish architects who practised in this country and in Britain for over a hundred years. Of Scottish descent, they came to Cork from the North of Ireland where they originally settled. The founder of the firm was Sir Thomas Deane (1792-1871). He was born in Cork, where his father, Alexander Deane, was an architect/builder. On his father's death he succeeded to the business. As he was then only fourteen years of age, his mother played a prominent part in the affairs of the firm, assisted, no doubt, by her other sons, Alexander and Kearns, both of whom died comparatively young. Thomas, the eldest, turned to architecture rather than contracting. He designed a number of buildings in the South and also

FORMER
KILDARE STREET
CLUB PREMISES,
KILDARE STREET.
CAPITALS AT
WINDOW HEAD.

The Kildare Street Club was founded in 1859 and the brick and stone building, on the corner of Kildare Street and South Leinster Street, was designed by Deane and Woodward and constructed in the 1860s. The building is now divided between the Alliance Française Cultural Centre and the Geneological Office. The original elaborate staircase was removed in 1954 but carvings by Charles W. Harrison still remain.

A special feature of the decorative exterior are the carvings at the bottom of the deep-set ground-floor windows.

DETAIL OF
CARVED
BASE TO
TWIN
COLUMNS.
IN THE
FORMER
PREMISES
OF THE
KILDARE
STREET
CLUB,
KILDARE
STREET.

took an interest in local affairs. He became High Sheriff of Cork in 1815, 1830 and again in 1851, and was knighted in 1830 on the occasion of a visit to that city by the Duke of Northumberland, Lord Lieutenant of Ireland.

Not much is known about Benjamin Woodward's early life. He was born in Tullamore in 1816. Apprenticed to an engineer or surveyor, he became interested in, and acquired a knowledge of architecture, and a special interest in medieval art. He was one of the architects who were influenced by the theories of John Ruskin (1819-1900). The basis of Ruskin's teaching lay in defining conditions of architectural beauty. He endeavoured to trace these back, in nearly every case, to the examples of nature. When these conditions were applied to actual buildings Ruskin's concern was for wall surface and texture, colour, carvings, light and shade, rather than for the organization of space or function. Ruskin believed these qualities were expressed more fully in medieval architecture than in the classical style. He advocated, in particular, the Lombardic-Venetian style of Northern Italy, which he favoured above others. In his advocacy, Ruskin went further than Pugin. He suggested the use of medieval art as a universal style suitable for secular as well as religious structures. Ruskin's teaching, which was put into practice by Woodward, influenced much of the work of the mid-century.

Sir Thomas Newenham Deane was the only son of old Sir Thomas. After a pupilage in his father's office, he entered into partnership with him and Benjamin Woodward about 1850. Shortly afterwards the firm moved to Dublin, where it practised under the title of Sir Thomas Deane, Son and Woodward. In 1854 they won the competiton for the Museum of Science at Oxford University. Woodward's design was one of the first fruits of Ruskin's teachings in England. It had, however, a predecessor in Ireland, the Museum, now the School of Engineering, in Trinity College. This was Woodward's first important building in Dublin. Begun in 1852, it was built on foundations laid by J S McCurdy, a Dublin architect. In the plan of the building the rooms are grouped around a fine top-lighted entrance hall with a great staircase. What is new is the polychromatic decoration of the interior. The design of the building, in the Lombardic-Venetian style, was influenced not only by Ruskin, but also by the work of Sir Charles Barry, one of the leading English architects of the day. The beautiful stonework, the rich naturalistic carvings by the gifted Cork sculptors, the O'Shea brothers, the decisive quality of the facades, with their great round-headed windows, the exposed roof and fine chimney stacks, make this building an outstanding example of 19th century revivalist architecture, and places Woodward among the foremost architects of his time in Ireland, if not in Britain. He discovered and encouraged the talented Cork sculptors, James and John O'Shea, who followed him to England to work on the carvings of the Oxford Museum, where their work did much to restore Ruskin's confidence in the genius of the unassisted workman.

The last important building by Woodward was the Kildare Street Club (1858). The site called for an urban treatment, which Woodward achieved by setting the building back behind an area and using brick in keeping with 18th century Dublin. The scale and proportions of the facades, almost cliff-like in appearance, have a dignity that

NATIONAL MUSEUM (NATURAL HISTORY), UPPER MERRION STREET.

The Natural History Division of the National Museum is located on the south side of Leinster Lawn, balacing the National Gallery of Ireland on the north side. Designed by Frederick V. Clarendon, it was finished in 1857. In front of the building is a statue of Surgeon Thomas H. Parke (an explorer and member of the Stanley Expedition) by Percy Wood, erected in 1896.

The Zoological Society was founded in 1830 and the Zoological Gardens were set up in the Phoenix park in 1831.

The Science and Art Museum, designed in the Classical manner by Sir Thomas Manly Deane, was completed in 1889. Art Collections of the Royal Dublin Society, the Royal Irish Academy and the Royal Society of Antiquaries of Ireland were transferred to the building in Kildare Street and the Museum, now the National Museum, was inaugurated in 1890. The Museum buildings, faced with Mount Charles sandstone, did not weather well in the city atmosphere.

The National Library, Kildare Street, was also designed by Sir Thomas Manly Deane and built at the same time as the Museum.

NATIONAL MUSEUM (SCIENCE AND ART), KILDARE STREET.

few buildings of the period can match. The stone columns and contrasting coloured brickwork lend interest, but are subservient to the general design. Many of the carvings were the work of Harrison, a Dublin sculptor. In the interior, the fine entrance hall, or court, with its great staircase, was altered when the building was changed to commercial use.

These buildings, Irish and English, established Woodward and the Deanes among the foremost architects of the day. Further work at Oxford, as well as commissions in London and elsewhere, came their way. Woodward, however, did not live long to enjoy the rewards. He died in 1861 aged 46.

Apart from the facade of St Ann's Church, Dawson Street, and the adjoining Parochial Hall and school (1857), now gone from Molesworth Street, the firm was also responsible for important commercial work in Dublin. The Scottish Widows Insurance Building, built of warm red Runcorn sandstone imported from Britain, occupies a prominent position at the corner of Westmoreland Street and College Street. The scale and treatment of this block designed in the Romanesque style owes much to its careful details, and is a good example of a 19th century office block, which fits in with its surroundings and is distinctive without being aggressive in design. These buildings set a fashion for Romanesque architecture which persisted in Dublin for a decade or so.

The third generation to join the firm was Thomas Manly Deane, the eldest son of Sir T N Deane. Born in 1851, he was apprenticed to William Burges of London, one of the leading spirits of the Gothic Revival. While in London, Deane won a scholarship offered by the Royal Academy School, of which he was a pupil. This encouraged him to travel abroad, where he acquired a knowledge of classical architecture and, in particular, that of the Italian Renaissance to which he remained faithful in most of his buildings. His work with Burges also left him well acquainted with medieval architecture, as may be seen in the old Commercial Union Insurance building (now No. 45), Dame Street, which, in conjunction with his father, he designed in the Romanesque style. The most important work of the partnership — the National Library of Ireland and the Science and Art Museum, Kildare Street — was not, however, in the medieval style, but in the classical manner, and belongs to a later period.

During the decades following the mid-century, medieval architecture persisted, although occasionally challenged by classical designs. A great variety of buildings, mainly in the former style, were erected in the city and its environs. Among the most important of the commercial structures were banks. A fine example is the old Hibernian (now Northern) Bank at the corner of Church Lane, College Green, designed in the Italian Romanesque style by William George Murray, about 1864. The original building, with its great arched windows recalling the earlier work by Woodward at Trinity College, consisted of four bays to College Green and two bays to Church Lane. This was later extended first by Sir Thomas Drew and again, in this century, by W H Byrne and Son, both architects continuing the original design.

FACADE,
SOUTH
CITY
MARKETS,
SOUTH
GREAT
GEORGE'S
STREET.

The competition for the design of the South City Markets was won by Lockwood and Mason of Bradford, England. The Markets were opened in 1881 but they were damaged by fire and reconstructed in 1892. Internal alterations were made in 1955 and further alterations were carried out in 1982. The building is faced with red brick and has decorative Gothic details. Brick facades adjoining the markets were designed by Henry Aaron Baker and he received an award for this work from th e Wide Streets Commissioners.

GOTHIC DETAILS,
SOUTH CITY MARKETS,
DRURY STREET,
FADE STREET.

Murray also designed the head office of the old Provincial Bank (c.1865), now Allied Irish Bank, College Street. The main feature of the building is the fine top-lighted cash office or banking hall. This splendid interior, in which Sir Thomas Drew, who was then Murray's assistant, had a hand, comes as a surprise after the rather timid treatment of the facade. The most interesting part of the exterior is the carved pediment by Samuel Lynn (brother of W H Lynn, the Belfast architect). This represents the Guardian of Banking as the central figure, supported on the left by the Spirit of Commerce and Manufacture and on the right by that of Agriculture, with minor figures making up a composition which, like the interior treatment, is a worthy successor to the great Renaissance traditions of the city. Somewhat later was the Northern Bank, Grafton Street, designed in the Italian Renaissance style by W H Lynn (Lanyon and Lynn, Belfast). The selection of this style, while reflecting susceptibilities regarding the propriety of Gothic, demonstrates Lynn's skill in this medium. The Banking Hall, was, as orginally designed, better than the exterior. Nevertheless, Ruskin's doctrine that Gothic could be used as a universal style, coupled with some influential English competitions such as that won by Deane and Woodward for the design of the Oxford Museum (begun 1854), ensured that for the next few decades Gothic would be the acceptable style for secular buildings in England and Ireland.

Typical of these Gothic adaptations to commercial use is the South City Markets, South Great Georges Street. Rebuilt in 1892 after a fire, it is an imposing red brick structure, dating from 1878, when the architects, Lockwood and Mason of Bradford, England, won a competition for the design of the building. The facades show the application of Gothic details to an excellent composition which occupies a whole block and still forms an important part of the street facade. The interior courtyard, once roofed over, sheltered the market stalls.

In contrast, the building forming the corner of D'Olier Street and Westmoreland Street, built as insurance offices and designed by the local architect, J J O'Callaghan. Completed in 1894 it is a large and elaborate stonework block, located in an important position.   It stands out, not only on account of its size and position, but also on account of the complexity of its treatment in what was largely simple brick surroundings comprising standard facades and shop fronts, designed about 1800 by Aaron Baker for the Wide Streets Commissioners. J J O'Callaghan also designed some churches, but his practice was mainly in commercial work, usually built of brickwork, designed in his own personal style which he adapted from medieval sources. His buildings included McKenzies Store (destroyed by fire and replaced by Oisin House), Pearse Street, the Old Dolphin Hotel (1887), Essex Street and O'Callaghan's, Dame Street. He also designed the O'Brien Institute, Malahide Road, a particularly strident example of red brickwork. This, and his office block at O'Connell Bridge, represent High Victorian architecture in an exuberance of colour and ornament which replaced the relative simplicity and sensitivity of Deane and Woodward. Although O'Callaghan studied with the firm, and worked on the Kildare Street Club and the Museum at Trinity College Dublin, and was clerk of works on the Oxford Union Building, he was, apparently, not greatly influenced by their example. His work also includes Mooney's pub (now Bruxelles), Harry Street, off

RATHMINES TOWN HALL

Rathmines became an independent township in 1847. The Town Hall was designed by Sir Thomas Drew for the Rathmines and Rathgar Urban District Council and was built in 1894. It is faced with red sandstone and has a Romanesque facade.

Pembroke became an independent township in 1853. The Pembroke Hall, Ballsbridge, was designed by Edward Henry Carson for the Pembroke Urban District Council. It has Gothic features and sandstone dressings.

The Urban District Councils were abolished in 1930 and both buildings are now used by the City of Dublin Vocational Education Committee.

The Rathmines Urban District Council, with the aid of a generous grant from Andrew Carnegie, LL.D., built the Public Library on the opposite side of the road to the Town Hall. The Library and the adjoining Technical Institute were built on a site at the corner of Leinster Road. The Library, designed by Batchelor and Hicks, was opened in 1913. A three-storey building, it is faced with terra cotta and red brick. There is a full entablature and balustraded parapet. A fleche rises from the roof.

Leinster Road, which runs from Rathmines to Harold's Cross, was opened in 1835 and Leinster Square was developed about the same time.

RATHMINES TOWN HALL

Grafton Street, with its fine interior. St Mary's Church (c.1895), Haddington Road, is a rather tame example of his church work.

Public buildings of the period included the town halls. These were used for the affairs of the townships; Clontarf, Pembroke, Rathmines, etc. When these districts were incorporated in the city proper, the buildings became redundant or were converted to other uses. In scale they varied in size and importance, from the relatively small and simple brick hall and rooms at Clontarf, to the large and impressive Rathmines Town Hall, designed by Sir Thomas Drew (1894). In his treatment of the building, erected on a rather inadequate site, he relied on both composition and materials, the high clock tower of red sandstone acting as a distinguishing feature. The Romanesque facade now appears rather grandiose or exotic in its surroundings. Internally the building was simpler in design, but the treatment has been altered substantially to meet the requirements of the City of Dublin Vocational Education Committee. The old Pembroke Town Hall at Ballsbridge now serves as offices for the same Committee. Built of local granite, with sandstone dressings, the design is an adaptation of basic Gothic features, such as the windows, to suit the nature of the stone. As such it is commendable, but it owes more to its site and setting than to its actual design. The architect was Edward Henry Carson, who was born in Dublin of Italian descent. His name today is overshadowed by that of his famous son, Edward. J L Robinson, a pupil of Carson, designed Dún Laoghaire Town Hall, which, in its treatment, recalls the manner of his master, but in a rather more pretentious way. Robinson was also the architect of the old portion of St Michael's Hospital (1876), as well as the Priory (1885) attached to the Dominican Church, Dominick Street.

A number of the Dublin hospitals were commenced in the 19th century: the Adelaide (1830); City of Dublin (1832); Coombe (1828); the Fever Hospital (1804), Cork Street; Mater (1861); Sir Patrick Dun's (1809) and St Vincent's (1834). Others, such as Jervis Street, the Meath, the Rotunda, Mercers, Steeven's, belong to the previous century. The new foundations were partly the outcome of a greater concern for treatment of disease and a growing awareness of the benefits of public health, coupled with the expansion and growth of the city.

The pavilion type of hospital plan, consisting of isolated ward blocks linked by a connecting corridor, as developed in Britain, did not find much favour in Irish planning. There are few examples, as Irish practice tended at the time to retain wards lighted and ventilated along one side only, with the beds facing each other and at right angles to the walls. This provided a more compact and tightly knit arrangement compared with the other layout.

The development of the city northwards along the line of, and in districts adjacent to, the North Circular Road, led to the opening of the Mater Misericordiae Hospital by the Sisters of Mercy in 1861. The original central block, containing forty beds, with its fine classical portico and steps, was designed by John Bourke, a Dublin architect, who also added the East Wing in 1871. It is of interest that in the course of the work Bourke visited hospitals in other countries, so testifying to the spirit

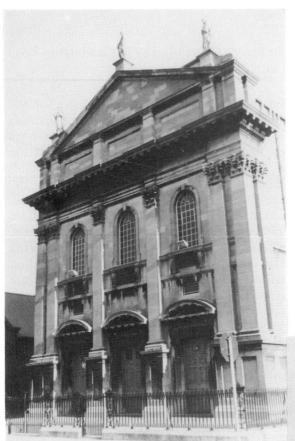

ST. AGATHA'S CHURCH, NORTH WILLIAM STREET.

St. Agatha's Church, North William Street, designed by William H. Byrne, was opened in 1908. It has a lofty aisleless nave and a spacious apse. In 1865 the surrounding district was formed into a separate parish.

Schools had already been built in the district by the Irish Christian Brothers and the French Sisters of Charity.

The Church of St. Laurence O'Toole was built in 1851 on a triangular site at Seville Place, as a chapel of ease to the Pro-Cathedral and two years later the Parish of St. Laurence O'Toole was constituted. The Gothic-style Church was designed by J. B. Keane and the tower and spire by John Bourke. The first stone of the nearby school was laid in 1847.

ST. LAURENCE O'TOOLE'S CHURCH, SEVILLE PLACE, NORTH WALL.

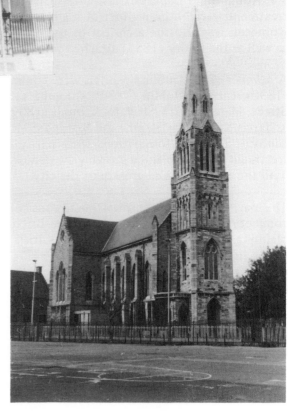

which animated the architect and the Sisters in their work. John Bourke died in 1871. He was also architect for Holy Cross Seminary, Clonliffe Road; the Dominican Convent, Cabra; and the spire of St Laurence O'Toole's (1858), the great Liffeyside church originally designed by John Keane, who was also associated with the Church of St Francis Xavier (1832), Gardiner Street. Bourke, like Keane, bridged the gap between the decline of the Irish Renaissance and the flowering of the Gothic Revival, by building in both styles. St Vincent's Hospital, prior to its move in 1970 to Elm Park, Merrion, was accommodated by adapting and extending a series of houses at St Stephen's Green, where it flourished for over one hundred years. These houses have now been replaced by an office block the frontage of which retains the external features of Georgian design.

Towards the end of the century, apart from technical improvements, changes of an aesthetic nature also occured in hospital design. This may be seen in the work of Albert Edward Murray (1849-1924) as the simplicity of earlier work yielded to a more varied treatment. A E Murray, a grandson of William Murray I, Johnston's partner, enjoyed an extensive practice working mainly in Dublin. He acted as consultant to many of the city hospitals, and built the Plunkett-Cairns wing (1895) to the Rotunda Hospital; the Nurses' home, Adelaide Hospital (1885), as well as the present front of the City of Dublin Hospital, Baggot Street. These buildings show a marked departure from the stone facades of his father's time. A E Murray preferred a more colourful treatment consisting of shiny red brick with yellow Ruabon terracotta (baked earth) panels and dressings, a combination of colours and textures which often appear garish and mechanical in effect. These hard and colourful materials were often used with little regard for their surroundings, and gave late 19th century architecture an individuality which distinguishes it today. Associated, but not forming part of the hospitals, were the Schools of Medicine, often directed and attended by eminent practitioners such as Sir William Wilde. A survival of these is the old Carmichael School in Aungier Street (now offices) designed in an over-elaborate free classical style, which incorporated pointed arches and other elements of medieval design, making a rather restless composition. A E Murray is said to have had a hand in the design of these typical brick and terracotta facades.

In the seventies and eighties, changes were taking place in the design of shops and stores. As in London, shopping arcades made their appearance at this time in Dublin, the unobtrusive small-paned windows were giving way to large sheets of plate glass, sheltering more spacious and better-lighted interiors. The abolition (1845) of duties on glass encouraged improvements in manufacture, and made large sheets possible at economic prices. Developments in building construction permitted larger spans. Department stores accommodating a variety of goods under one roof came into fashion. Typical of these were McKenzies great store in Pearse Street, with open galleries approached by wide stairs. In domestic and semi-domestic work the so-called skeleton sash window became popular. This consisted of single sheets of glass filling the entire upper and lower sashes, replacing what was now considered to be the old-fashioned Georgian panes.

STATUE OF QUEEN VICTORIA.

The bronze statue of Queen Victoria which stood in front of Leinster House from 1907 to 1948 was the work of sculptor John Hughes. The 4.5 m high figure which stood on a 5 m high plinth of Sicilian marble was surrounded by figures representing fame, art, literature and science. After its removal from Leinster House, the statue of Queen Victoria was first brought to the Royal Hospital, Kilmainham, then to Daingean Reformatory and finally it was donated by the Government to the Lord Mayor of Sydney.

A statue of Prince Albert, husband of Queen Victoria, by John Henry Foley, was erected on Leinster Lawn in 1871. It is surrounded by figures of an artist, a shepherd, a mechanic and a photographer.

The Nelson Pillar was erected in O'Connell Street (then known as Sackville Street) in 1808-09. The granite Doric column, 40 m high, was designed by W. Wilkins, with Francis Johnston as consultant architect. The statue of Nelson was executed by Thomas Kirk. The porch, by G. P. Beater, was added in 1894. The Pillar was destroyed in 1966.

DEMOLITION
OF NELSON
PILLAR,
O'CONNELL
STREET.

Similar developments, involving plate glass, were apparent in 19th century hotels. Improvements in transport, greater wealth and commercial enterprise gave rise to the provision of more luxurious accommodation for travellers. The Shelbourne Hotel, St Stephen's Green, was altered and extended at this time by the local architect, J S McCurdy, who remodelled the interior and added the present ornate frontages about 1866. He was also the architect for the Royal Marine Hotel at Dún Laoghaire, both typical of solid Victorian comfort and prestige.

The most important city buildings of the second half of the century were the National Library of Ireland and the Science and Art Museum, Kildare Street, to which reference has already been made. These were won in competition by the Deanes. They were designed mainly by Thomas Manly Deane, whose taste for the Italian Renaissance style brought classical architecture to the fore after a lapse of twenty or so years. Their convex layout on both sides of Leinster House, and their elaborate treatment, internally and externally, indicate Deane's mastery of momumental design, and recalls the influence of the Ecole des Beaux Arts, Paris, rather than the simple native Renaissance style of which Leinster House is an early example.

The Library, in particular, is an exercise in harmonious planning. The relationship between hall, staircase and reading room is pleasant and direct, even if the scale of the first is diminutive compared with the other two. The reading room, which is rather more than a semi-circle in plan, is the climax of an internal layout of great dignity. Its shape was obviously influenced by that of the British Museum. Unfortunately the exterior of the buildings was marred by the use of an unsuitable stone; the Mount Charles sandstone from Co Donegal, used as a facing, decayed in the city atmosphere and has been gradually replaced by Portland stone.

The Deanes also designed (1907 approx) an elaborate pedestal for the statue of Queen Victoria, which formerly stood between these buildings and in front of Leinster House. This statue by John Hughes, an Irish sculptor, was, on account of the rather grim and disapproving facial expression of Her Majesty, popularly known as "Ireland's Revenge", until its removal to make way for a hard landscape. The Deanes also designed the Lecture Theatre in Leinster House for the Royal Dublin Society. This later became the Chamber of Dáil Éireann.

Thomas Manly Deane, who died in retirement of 1933, was the last member of the firm established by his grandfather in Cork in the early years of the 19th century. His grandfather, old Sir Thomas, was knighted in 1830, his father, Thomas Newenham, was knighted in 1888, on the occasion of the opening of the Kildare Street buildings, and in 1911 Thomas Manly was himself knighted by King George V, the third successive Deane to get such recognition, unique in an Irish architectural family.

The name of Sir Charles Cameron, the City Medical Officer, should be mentioned for his efforts to improve the sanitary conditions of the city, its water supply, sewerage and housing. In this he was a worthy follower of Chadwick, the pioneer of

OLYMPIA THEATRE, DAME STREET.

In 1879 Dan Lowry's Star of Erin Music Hall was reconstructed, with a new front in Dame Street, and renamed the Empire Theatre of Varieties. It was also known as the Palace. Both these names appear on the glazed entrance canopy. Above the canopy the more recently adopted name is prominently displayed.

On the opposite side of the street there is a shop premises designed by J. J. O'Callaghan.

In 1904 the Abbey Theatre opened in the former Mechanics Institute building, adapted by the Dublin architect, Joseph Holloway.

The original Theatre Royal was built in 1812. It was damaged by fire in 1886 and reconstructed in 1897. The third Theatre Royal was opened in 1935 as a cine-variety theatre. It closed in 1962 and was replaced by the Hawkins House office block.

The Gaiety Theatre, South King Street, opened by M. Gunn in 1871, was overhauled and refurbished in 1896 and again a number of times subsequently. It has a Baroque interior and a yellow brick facade. The original design was by J. C. Phipps, London.

GAIETY THEATRE, SOUTH KING STREET.

Public Health legislation in England. The Vartry supply, with its great reservoir of pure water, dated from 1863-8, but the main drainage systems were not laid until between 1902 and 1906. These replaced the cesspools and old sewers discharging into the Liffey, causing unpleasant pollution. It may be of interest to recall that the house supply pipes used for the Vartry water were an alloy of lead and tin called "Vartry Metal". Pure lead pipes were too soft, as the metal tended to dissolve in the soft water. The use of this special piping lasted well into this century, when copper tubing rendered it obsolete. Plastic piping was introduced later.

The population of the city and suburbs (248,000 in 1891) called for changes in the marketing of food. The present Vegetable Market in Mary's Lane was, for instance, built in 1892, to serve the needs of the municipal area then stretching mainly between the North and South Circular Roads and the canals. The major expansion of the city beyond the limits did not begin until the 1920s. The layout of these great markets, in contrast to the Market Halls of the early part of the century, reflect the developments in building construction, particularly the use of cast iron and glass, which made large open spans and top lighting possible.

Some other types of buildings deserve mention, as they represent the material, if not the artistic, progress of the 19th century. Ever since the days of Classical Greece, theatres and theatre going were one of the amenities of urban life. The 19th century was no exception, particularly in the adaptation of modern construction and services which rendered stagecraft more realistic and the auditoriums more spacious and comfortable. The only 19th century theatres remaining are the Gaiety (1871, by J C Phipps, London) and the Olympia (1879). The Gate is housed in 18th century assembly rooms, while the Royal, Tivoli and Queens were destroyed. The Rotunda and the Antient Concert Rooms, Brunswick Street (now Pearse Street) are cinemas. The original Abbey was opened in 1904, when the old Mechanics Institute, Abbey Street, was adapted by the Dublin architect and theatre-goer, Joseph Holloway, its sombre auditorium contrasting with the gay and handsome interiors of the other city theatres.

In complete contrast are the prisons of the period. Kilmainham Jail, architecturally the finest, is said to have been designed by Sir John Traille, High Sheriff of Dublin. It was completed in 1796, so that, architecturally, it belongs to the Greek Revival style of the late 18th century, with some 19th century alterations by John S McCurdy. The main influence on prison planning in this country came from England, where, in the 19th century, the views of John Howard and others had an important bearing on prison layout. After the abolition of transportation, increased prison accommodation was required. Mountjoy Prison (1849) is a grim and joyless conception based on Pentonville Prison, London. The plan takes into account the principles of penal reform which were mainly related to the separation and close supervision of prisoners. The plans are noted as having been prepared by Major Jebb, and completed in London with the permission of the Irish Board of Works.

LIFFEY VIEW LOOKING WEST FROM ROSSA BRIDGE

The view from O'Donovan Rossa Bridge (formerly Richmond Bridge), built in 1813, shows the silhouette of Father Mathew Bridge (formerly the Whitworth Bridge). The Wellington Testimonial can be seen above the central arch of the bridge and St. Paul's Church, Arran Quay, can be seen on the right.

The Wellington Bridge, Liffey Bridge, or Ha'penny Bridge as it is popularly known, is a graceful cast iron structure. Erected through the enterprise of Lord Beresford and William Walsh, it was a toll bridge as the nickname implies, but no charge has been made since 1919. The bridge was made by the Coalbrookdale Foundry, Shopshire, England.

A table of Liffey Bridges is printed on page 82 and six of them are illustrated on pages 178 and 179.

This metal foot-bridge is 3.7 wide.

HA'PENNY BRIDGE

CIVIC IMPROVEMENTS AND PUBLIC MONUMENTS

After the Union, as Dublin declined in wealth and influence, it sought to gain other advantages, principally in municipal improvements. In the early part of the 19th century the police force was reformed, gas lighting introduced and the water supply extended to serve new suburbs. In the suburbs the influence of the Wide Street Commissioners is still apparent. Morehampton Road, Leinster Road, Waterloo Road, Rathmines Road, are all impressive thoroughfares, although the latter has been subjected to commercial encroachment. On the North side the linking of Dorset Street, the North Circular Road, Gardiner Street and Mountjoy Street by some new connecting streets, also came about, but on a much reduced scale. Sherrard Street Lower and Upper (1825) suggests the date and recalls the name of the last two surveyors/secretaries to the Commissioners before they were abolished in 1841, when their functions were taken over by the Corporation.

With new developments, North and South of the Liffey, communications between the two sides of the city were improved. New bridges were built, such as the Whitworth (now Father Mathew Bridge), in 1816. This was sited between Bridgefoot Street and Church Street, and occupies the approximate position of the "Old Bridge", the original Dublin bridge of timber, first built in 1215, later rebuilt, and for centuries the only crossing over the Liffey. Improvements were also made to existing bridges. The most important was the reconstruction of O'Connell Bridge, formerly known as Carlisle Bridge, replacing Gandon's design of 1791. This was widened, rebuilt and reopened in 1880. Although it appears to be a stone bridge (reusing Gandon's balustrades), the main structure is of cast iron designed by Bindon Blood Stoney, a Dublin engineer. This rebuilding hastened the change in the character of O'Connell Street, then known as Sackville Street, from that of a fashionable residential street to a business area.

Some sixty-five years earlier, in 1816, the Wellington (Metal) Bridge was opened, a graceful cast iron structure with a clear span of approximately sixty metres. This was a pioneer work and early example of the use of cast iron in structural design. Formerly known as "the Ha-penny Bridge", the toll of ½d for pedestrians was abolished about sixty years ago.

George Papworth (1781-1855), who came to this country from England about 1806, designed Kingsbridge (now Heuston Bridge) in 1822, using cast iron to form a single span of about thirty metres. It was a splendid achievement and the subject of many engravings. A vehicular crossing, it is of historic and practical value, rather than of aesthetic interest. Papworth prospered in this country, where he built up an extensive practice. He influenced the domestic architecture of the early 19th century, and is credited with the stucco fronted Regency type of Georgian terraced house, as in Upper Leeson Street, Dún Laoghaire, Monkstown, etc. He is also said to have introduced the broad entrance steps of granite, which became a feature of Dublin

Towards the end of the Eighteenth Century Harcourt Street and Camden Street were developed. The houses on the right were built in the Nineteenth Century. The street retains much of its original character although individual buildings have been replaced and others altered to meet changes in use. Clonmell House (1778), the tallest building on the left, housed the Municipal Gallery between 1908 and 1929, after which it was moved to Charlemont House, Parnell Square, now the Sir Hugh Lane Municipal Gallery of Modern Art.

An attractive feature of Harcourt Street is its gentle curve. The green copper dome of Rathmines Church closes the vista as one looks down the street in a southerly direction. The Children's Hospital, originally founded in 1821 as the Institution for Sick Children, is on the left.

Cardinal Newman, founder of the Catholic University of Ireland, resided in Harcourt Street during his stay in Dublin.

HARCOURT STREET, LOOKING TOWARDS RATHMINES.

houses later in the century. He also designed the fine classical sarcophagus (1817) marking John Philpott Curran's grave in Glasnevin Cemetery.

Butt Bridge, also by Stoney, opened in 1878, was the last of the 19th century bridges. It was a cramped and ugly metal swivel bridge, replaced about 1933 by the present structure built to ease traffic congestion. The Loop Line Railway, completed in 1891, proved to be a visual disaster.

Apart from its structural use, the ironwork of the 19th century includes some splendid examples of ornamental gates and railings. Typical are the railings around Trinity College, designed by McCurdy; also the gates and boundary chains of the old Exhibition Buildings in Earlsfort Terrace. These chains of alternating links and balls, are still in position, suspended between iron finials, while the gates with clenched gauntlets as hinges, are sturdy and robust in both design and construction. These and other examples in both city and suburbs, show iron used to decorative advantage. Cast work based on the Greek honeysuckle ornament may be seen as a roof cresting in the Botanic Gardens.

In the 18th century much of the fashionable life of the city was centred in the gardens and assembly rooms of the period. After the Union an attempt was made to revive these gatherings when, in 1817, the Coburg Gardens were opened in the grounds of Clonmel House, Harcourt Street. Afterwards the gardens formed the site of the Exhibitions of 1865 and 1872, and are now incorporated in the Iveagh Gardens. The Exhibition of 1872 was devoted to the Arts, Industries and Manufactures. It was promoted by Sir Arthur and his brother, Edward Cecil Guinness, afterwards Lords Iveagh and Ardilaun respectively, and held in the Exhibition Buildings of 1865.

Nineteenth century garden design was based on two contrasting styles, formal and landscape. The formal treatment goes back to the Italianate gardens of the 17th century, and introduced into England by Sir Charles Barry (1795-1875), and thence to Ireland. Powerscourt, Co. Wicklow, although outside Dublin, is near enough to be mentioned as Ireland's finest formal gardens, laid out (1843-1875) in the grand manner with terraces, steps, urns, etc. set in a splendid landscape, where the Sugarloaf Mountains terminate the view. It was designed, in part, by Daniel Robertson, an English architect, who came to Dublin about 1830.

Landscape gardens continued the traditions of the 18th century. This type of informal or "natural" layout, was pioneered during the 19th century in this country by, among others, William Robertson, who was born in Ireland in 1833 of poor parents. He was trained as a gardener in this country, but while working in England he educated himself and became a writer as well as a practitioner. His vision was of natural gardens as opposed to formal or artificial ones, and this was widely accepted as an alternative to the elaborate formal gardens which required much care and maintenance. The grounds of St Anne's, Clontarf, with its mixture of the exotic, may be regarded as an example of Robertson's ideas. In contrast, the gardens at the

ÁRAS AN UACHTARÁIN IONIC PORTICO BY FRANCIS JOHNSTON who also designed the Doric portico on the other side of the building.

What was originally a ranger's house built in 1745 in the Phoenix Park was later used as the residence of the Viceroy and it finally became Áras an Uachtaráin in 1938, the residence of the President of Ireland. Many alterations and additions to the building have been carried out from time to time. Francis Johnston was the architect responsible for the wings which were added in 1816 and for the portico built about the same time. Other extensions were carried out in 1848 and in 1911 additional bedrooms were built. The gardens were laid out by Decimus Burton and he also designed the lodges.

The Polo Pavilion, a short distance from Áras an Uachtaráin, was built in 1872.

The Phoenix Park was opened to the public in the middle of the Eighteenth Century. The Park gate lodges, built about 1808, were designed by Decimus Burton. The Nineteenth Century stone gate piers removed from the main entrance in 1932 have been reinstated.

ÁRAS AN UACHTARÁIN, PHOENIX PARK.

Vice-Regal Lodge (now Aras an Uachtaráin), are in the formal manner. These were laid out about 1840 by the English architect, Decimus Burton (1800-1881), who also designed the lodges and carried out other improvements in the Park.

The Zoological Gardens (1830) were enclosed and laid out in an informal manner around an artificial lake, an arrangement which may have influenced the treatment of St Stephen's Green later in the century. The Green, eleven hectares in extent, was laid out by English gardeners at the expense and under the direction of Lord Ardilaun. The gates and piers were designed by J F Fuller, a local architect, while the ornate gate lodge at the Harcourt Street corner is a good example of careful workmanship. The Fusiliers' Memorial Arch at Grafton Street belongs to the 20th century.

A feature of some 19th century gardens were the great conservatories of glass and metal construction. The Palm House in the Botanic Gardens, Glasnevin, is an excellent example of a large-scale glasshouse, completed in 1846 by Fred Darley, a Dublin architect. It was built by the Dublin iron master, Richard Turner of Ballsbridge, a pioneer in metal structures. Decimus Burton may have had a hand in the design, as he worked in Dublin between 1834 and 1849 on the Phoenix Park developments, and also for the Earl of Howth. The Palm House, Kew Gardens (1844-48) and the Conservatory in Regents Park, London, were both designed by Burton. The ironwork for these was supplied by Turner, who had the sections made in Dublin and shipped to London for assembly. Turner was consulted by Paxton on the vault of the Crystal Palace, London (1851), after his own design was ruled out on the ground of cost. The Botanic Gardens were originally formed by the Royal Dublin Society in the closing decade of the 18th century. The last act of the Irish Parliament was a grant to the Society, part of which was used for their completion.

Apart from reclamation works along the shores of Dublin Bay and completion of the Bull Wall and bridge (c.1820), port facilities were improved and outlying harbours developed. Chief among these were Dún Laoghaire and Howth. From 1813 the latter was the terminal of the packet service to England. The road thence to the city was part of the London-Dublin road laid out by Thomas Telford (1757-1834), the great English engineer. However, with the transfer of the shipping service to Dún Laoghaire due to silting of Howth harbour, the latter and the road leading to it, declined in importance, while Dún Laoghaire grew from what was a small fishing village into a fine maritime resort. In the city a major improvement was the opening up of Lord Edward Street. This followed the restoration of Christ Church Cathedral (completed 1878), giving a direct approach from Cork Hill. Tara Street, connecting Great Brunswick Street (now Pearse Street) to Butt Bridge, was also laid out about this time.

Few of the public monuments of the 19th century still standing are of great architectural importance. A curious aspect of monumental design in Dublin was the popularity of the obelisk, a tall, slender rectangular shaft tapering to a point, a form that goes back to ancient Egypt, where obelisks were used to dignify the entrances to the temples and to mark important sites or boundaries. The most massive of the

WELLINGTON TESTIMONIAL, PHOENIX PARK.

Construction of the Wellington Testimonial in the Phoenix Park, designed by the English architect Sir Robert Smirke, was commenced in 1817, in honour of the Duke of Wellington. The architect was chosen as a result of a competition and the monument which he designed rises to a height of 60 m, the pedestal alone being 7 m high and 17 m square. The pictorial bronze relief panels were added in 1861.

An earlier and comparatively small obelisk at Newtown Park in Blackrock was designed by Edward Pearce and built in 1732 by Joshua Allen as a mausoleum for the Allen family.

The magazine, not far from Wellington Testimonial was constructed in 1801.

An obelisk designed by John Aird and erected in Dún Laoghaire in 1823 is in the form of a truncated granite pyramid standing on four granite balls. It commemorates the laying of the first stone of Dún Laoghaire Harbour.

The obelisk on Killiney Hill was erected for John Mapas in 1742 and the obelisk in James's Street was erected in 1789.

The small obelisk in the middle of road near Donnybrook Church was erected to the memory of Alderman Morrison, Lord Mayor of Dublin, who resided in the district.

OBELISK, DONNYBROOK.

Dublin obelisks is the Wellington Testimonial, Phoenix Park, begun in 1817 by the English architect, Sir Robert Smirke (1781-1867). Originally it was intended for St Stephen's Green, but happily the proposal fell through as its great height, over sixty-two metres (the equivalent of a seventeen storey building of today) would have been out of scale in such surroundings. The obelisk again appears at Donnybrook, but on a much reduced scale, as well as in the monument at Dún Laoghaire commemorating the visit of George IV and his departure from that harbour in 1821. Incidentally a further example is the Collins-Griffith Memorial designed by Raymond McGrath, erected on the Leinster Lawn in the middle of the present century. The Parnell Monument, Upper O'Connell Street, has a triangular shaped obelisk as a background to the figure. The name Obelisk Park, Blackrock, also refers to another of these monuments.

Of the statues that line O'Connell Street, once dominated by Nelson Pillar, the O'Connell Monument designed by Foley, has an heroic statue of the Liberator (3.7m high), while beneath are allegorical figures, the chief being Éire holding the Act of Emancipation, with winged figures representing Patriotism, Eloquence, Fidelity and Courage. This imaginative monument, commissioned in 1864, was completed after Foley's death by his assistant, Brock, and unveiled in 1882. John Henry Foley (1818-1874) was the most talented of the Irish sculptors of the period. The fine statues of Goldsmith (1864) and Burke (1868) in College Green, are his work, as also is the statue of Prince Albert in the London Memorial of that name.

The Campanile, Trinity College, was designed by Sir Charles Lanyon, Belfast, about 1853, and replaced the old College belfry. In its complexity it is typical of 19th century design, and although it lacks the repose of the older buildings of the College, it is an interesting and well-placed feature of the campus. Nearby is the Graduates' Memorial, a building designed by the local architect Sir Thomas Drew.

The great city cemeteries, Mount Jerome, Harold's Cross (1836) and Mount Prospect, Glasnevin, were acquired to replace the crowded parish graveyards. The most remarkable of their commemorative monuments is the O'Connell Tomb and Tower, Glasnevin, the latter based on the Irish Round Tower. This was only part of a plan put forward by George Petrie, who suggested that the monument should consist of a group of buildings, comprising a chapel based on Cormac's Chapel, Cashel, a celtic cross and a round tower. Only the latter was realised and completed by Early and Powell in 1869. O'Connell's remains were transferred to the vault under the tower. The cemetery lodge, railings and chapel were designed by J J McCarthy about 1878 to form a new entrance from Finglas Road.

Among the minor memorials were fountains, some of which served utilitarian as well as commemorative functions. An example still surviving is the Grattan Fountain (1880), St Stephen's Green, opposite Dawson Street, which provided refreshment for both man and beast. This — of medieval design carried out in polished granite — was to the design of the Deanes. The Crampton Memorial was another street fountain composed of quaint botanical forms, which caused it to be known as "the cauliflower".

RUTLAND FOUNTAIN, MERRION SQUARE.

The Rutland Fountain, Merrion Square West, designed by Francis Sandys, was erected in 1791. This memorial to the Duke of Rutland is decorated with urns from the works of Mrs. Coade in Lambeth who developed the technique of using terra cotta or artificial stone for making ornaments. The monument was restored in 1975 with the help of a fund set up in memory of Sybil Le Brocquy.

On the north side of Leinster Lawn, the garden of Leinster House, there is a statue of Sir Robert Stewart (1825-1894), composer and musician, who was a professor in the Royal Irish Academy of Music. The sculptor was Sir Thomas Farrell, PRHA, who also executed the statue of Lord Ardilaun erected in St. Stephen's Green in 1892.

STATUE OF SIR ROBERT STEWART, LEINSTER LAWN.

It commemorated Sir Philip Crampton MD (1777-1858), and was presented to the city by the Duke of Northumberland, a former Lord Lieutenant, as a tribute to Crampton's professional skill. It formerly stood at the junction of College Street, D'Olier Street and Pearse Street until it removal a decade or so ago. It was designed by William Vitruvius Morrison, with sculptures by Kirk. These fountains, however, cannot compare with the Rutland Memorial in Merrion Square, designed (1791) by Francis Sandys. The change in taste and the decline in architectural refinement in later work are evident.

The Statue of Father Theobald Mathew by John Henry Foley was erected in Upper O'Connell Street in 1890 to celebrate the centenary of the Temperance movement.

The marble statue of William Smith O'Brien, a leader of the 1848 Rising, was unveiled in 1870 and the statue of St. John Gray, associated with Dublin's Vartry water supply, was unveiled in 1879. Both of these statues are also in O'Connell Street.

STATUE OF
FR. THEOBALD MATHEW,
UPPER O'CONNELL STREET.

WINDOWS,
AIB,
7, DAME
STREET.

The Munster Bank was built on the corner of Dame Street and Palace Street in 1861 – 74 years later it became the Munster and Leinster Bank and more recently became part of the Allied Irish Banks Group. It is in the Italian Venetian style favoured by the architects Deane and Woodward and it was extended in the same style. The facade is of Ballinasloe limestone.

Benjamin Woodward was deeply involved in the design of the Museum building but he did not live to see the completion of the Bank in Dame Street.

The Museum, now the School of Engineering, Trinity College, designed by Deane and Woodward and built in 1854-57, has a wealth of fine architectural detail with superb stone carving by the O'Shea brothers. The fenestration was obviously given great consideration by the architects. It is interesting to compare the windows of the Museum building with those in the Dame Street Bank building illustrated above.

WINDOWS, MUSEUM (NOW SCHOOL OF ENGINEERING), TRINITY COLLEGE.

STRUCTURE AND MATERIALS

Pugin's dictum, "strength, utility and reality constitute beauty", seems to explain the structural qualities of Victorian buildings as well as to suggest their aesthetic ends. There are few hidden or novel aspects of 19th century construction. Structure was straightforward, based on the traditional use of brick and stone in heavy solid walling. In church work, stone was pre-eminent, but it did not always come from native sources. In the early part of the century the local calp (limestone) was used. Where of good quality it proved durable and weathered effectively, in varying shades of sombre grey. Calp was chiefly built in uncoursed random-sized rectangular blocks. The quality varied considerably; some stone was only suitable as a backing material protected from the weather, but good quality stone for facings was brought to the city from Lucan and Leixlip.

During the second half of the century calp stone fell out of favour, and granite came into general use. Granite was used as rubble (irregular) walling, in fairly small blocks finished with a rough or "rock" face, which gave brighter tones and more refracted surfaces than the calp stone. Granite, however, was on account of its coarse grain, generally unsuitable for carved works such as tracery, so that these type of details as well as jambs to doors and windows, were of smooth dressed limestone. This combination of rough and smooth surfaces proved to be both practical and effective. Many of the later churches of granite and limestone have weathered effectively even in the polluted areas of the city, where the granite has remained clean and sparkling.

Most of the granite used in the Dublin buildings came from the Ballyknockan quarries near Blessington, Co Wicklow. It was generally prepared by local masons and delivered almost ready for building. This made its use more economic than the stone from the Dublin quarries which, on account of hardness, made for difficulties in working. Dun Laoghaire Railway Station was built of stone brought from near Blessington rather than from the local granite which was used in the construction of the harbour piers. A typical example of Ballyknockan granite is St Paul's Church, Arran Quay. But the delicacy of the Greek mouldings has been lost in the texture of the stone. For secular work the fine Ballinasloe limestone was used to advantage, as, for instance, in the facades of the old Munster and Leinster Bank (now Allied Irish Bank) at the corner of Palace Street and Dame Street. The building (1873) was designed by the Deanes and has weathered well. The design with carved insets continued the fashion and recalls in general the treatment of the Trinity Museum some twenty years earlier.

Imported stones, particularly from North of England, were also used successfully in the Dublin atmosphere. Unlike Portland stone, these were mainly red and pink sandstones, used for their texture and colour. A good example is the old Scottish Widows Insurance Building at the corner of Westmoreland Street and College Street, designed by the Deanes and faced with Mansfield stone from Nottinghamshire. Caen stones from the North of France proved unsuitable for external use in Dublin, but

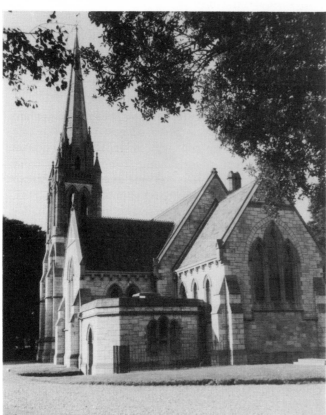

ALL SAINTS CHURCH, RAHENY.

The site for All Saints, Raheny, was donated by Edmund Arthur Guinness who also financed the building of the church, which was designed by Goerge Ashlin, architect, and erected in 1887. The walls are faced externally with granite and dressings are of limestone. Caen stone was chosen for use inside. The graceful spire rises to a height of 34 m.

St. Assam's Church, Raheny, designed by Patrick Byrne, architect, was blessed by Cardinal Cullen in 1864. It is no longer in use as a Church as a spacious new one was built on the opposite side of the road in 1962 to serve the large population now living in the parish.

St. Pappin's Church, Ballymun, was opened in 1848.

In 1830 the thatched chapel in Coolock was extended and a new slated roof constructed.

ST. ASSAM'S CHURCH, RAHENY.

both it and Bath stone from England were often used for internal carved work. The interior of All Saints Church, Raheny, is in Bath stone. Aberdeen granite was also imported as polished shafts for columns. These were often used in church work with Bath or Caen stone caps and bases. The contrast between the shiny reddish pink granite and the chalk white stone is generally harsh and unsympathetic.

Brick was cheaper than stone and more speedy to build. It was generally used around Dublin for secular work. At first local bricks from Crumlin, Dolphin's Barn, Portmarnock, etc. were in use as well as bricks from Athy, Tullamore, Kingscourt and Gorey. In England the mechanization of brick production in the sixties led to reduced costs, thus it became economic to import English brick. These machine-made bricks were almost identical in size, shape and colour. The mortar joints became thin and regular and the general effect was one of monotonous regularity. The dense shiny bricks of the period were also much favoured, and regarded as highly practical. The diapering of brickwork with coloured courses was not much used, but contrasting bands of stone as well as stone dressings, were used to divide large wall surfaces and to emphasise features of the design. Occassionally, as in the work of Albert Murray, glazed terra-cotta (baked earth) slabs were used in conjunction with brickwork, sometimes ornamented with cartouches (shields) strapworks, scrolls, etc. Shiny brickwork, terra-cotta, and highly glazed tiles came from England where they were used to resist dirt and pollution.

Elaborate patterns in glazed floor tiles were developed. Good examples of their use include the vestibule of the Allied Irish Bank, College Street, and the chancel of the All Hallows College Chapel, Dublin. Mosaic work was also commonly used, particularly in churches where the chancel floor was often laid out in decorative patterns. These mosaics were produced, not by craftsmen, but by mechanical means. They are generally dull and unattractive and have little in common, except in name, with the great mosaics of the past. Mosaic and tiling were, however durable materials easy to keep clean and, as such, had a strong practical appeal.

The normal roofing material was slate. Tiles did not come into fashion in this country until the 20th century. The 19th century roofs were generally exposed and more prominent than those of the 18th century, when they were generally hidden behind parapets and balustrades. In church work roofs were steeply sloped, with pitches up to 60°, finished with gables rather than hips. Slates from County Wicklow (the Earl of Fitzwilliam's quarries, near Ashford) were much used in Dublin. Bluish-grey in colour, they resembled thick Bangor (Wales) slates. In Irish work, slates, as well as being nailed, were usually rendered or plastered with hair and mortar on the underside. Later Welsh slates became popular, particularly the thin purple slates commonly known as "Blue Bangors". They were the joy of the late 19th and early 20th century Dublin builders as they were regular in shape, light in weight, long lasting and easy to lay or fix. Unlike some native varieties, they did not require sorting for size and thickness prior to roofing. Their defects were of an aesthetic nature; the colour was unpleasant, particularly when used with red brick. Moulded and ornamental chimney

PALM HOUSE,
BOTANIC
GARDENS,
GLASNEVIN.

The Great Palm House (1884) in the Botanic Gardens, Glasnevin, was designed by Frederick Darley and built by Richard Turner of Ballsbridge, an expert in iron-framed construction, who did outstanding work not only in Dublin but also in Belfast and London. The Curvilinear Range of iron-framed glasshouses (1843-69) in Glasnevin was constructed by Richard Turner. Duncan Ferguson, Frederick Darley and E. T. Owens all had an input into the design of the glasshouses but most of the credit for the final result must go to Richard Turner and his son, Sir William Turner.

The Royal Dublin Society opened the Botanic Gardens, which cover about 20 hectares, in 1795, "to foster the taste for practical and scientific botany". The gardens were handed over to the state in 1877.

CURVILINEAR
RANGE OF
GLASSHOUSES,
BOTANIC
GARDENS,
GLASNEVIN.

pots became a feature of 19th century roofs. These pots gave the chimney stacks unusual prominence.

The most striking advance in 19th century construction was the use of cast iron as a building material. Its structural use in this country dates from the early part of the 19th century, when it was used for isolated elements such as roof trusses and bridge spans. Its success was assured after the completion of the Crystal Palace, London (1851), later copied in Dublin for the Exhibition of 1865. It was, however, left to the engineers, British and Irish, to exploit the advantages of metal construction. Architects were more concerned about the ethics and aesthetics of the material which, for technical and economic reasons, could no longer be ignored. Ruskin's views on structure were about columns, walls, arches, texture, colour and surface richness. He was not concerned about problems of construction. Nevertheless, architects had to come to terms with this new material. One of the first attempts as Woodward's use of cast iron columns and beams in the Oxford Museum, with the decorative details such as the foliage of wrought or hand-forged iron added, or fixed separately, to the structural and decorative elements. In Ireland it was late in the century before the use of iron became general. Around 1890 the traditional timber floor beams were being replaced by cast iron beams. In the National Museum, Dublin, the ironwork supporting the roof and galleries is worthy of notice, if not of admiration.

Iron had practical limitations. These led to the development of steel as a structural material. Steel, like iron, was first used in bridge construction. The Forth Bridge, Edinburgh, opened 1890, was a major advance in steel construction, but steel was little used in building work in this country until the 20th century. The other outstanding building material in the 19th century was Portland cement, principally used in concrete. In this country, as well as in Britain, the development of reinforced concrete is associated with Francois Hennibique (1834-1921), but it was not widely used until the 20th century when, commonly called ferro-concrete, it was used in building works of public utility such as silos, factories, jetties, etc. The great advances in 20th century construction were the outcome of earlier experiments and studies during the 19th century in such subjects as the theory of structures and strength of materials. These mathematical concepts contributed to the growing division between the architect and the engineer, although earlier in the century an architect like Papworth could design an iron bridge as well as a mansion such as Kenure Park, Co Dublin. This spilt into separate professions was emphasised by the setting up of new engineering schools. The earliest was in Glasgow (1840), but Dublin quickly followed when Trinity College opened their engineering school in 1841, while those in the Queen's Colleges in Belfast, Cork and Galway came about fifteen years later.

In this country formal education for architects began in the 18th century in the Drawing School set up by the Dublin Society (now the RDS). Thomas Ivory, Aaron Baker and T J Papworth, all architects, were headmasters. In the 19th century classes in Building Construction, History of Architecture and Drawing were held in the Dublin Technical Schools and in the School of Art respectively. These classes were ancillary to the general acceptance of the pupilage system in which the aspiring

UNIVERSITY COLLEGE, EARLSFORT TERRACE.

The front boundary walls, chains and gates were part of the Exhibition complex, 1865.

The Exhibition Palace, Earlsfort Terrace, was adapted by Edward Kavanagh to the requirements of the Royal University in 1886-87. The commission for the design of University College was placed with R. M. Butler following an architectural competition held in 1912. It was built in 1914-19 but the original project was not completed with the result that some of the 1872 Dublin Exhibition buildings, designed by McCurdy, still remain as do also the front boundary wall, piers and gate. The Great Hall has been converted into An Ceoláras Náisiúnta/The National Concert Hall (1981). The University building, designed by R. M. Butler, is in the Greek Revival style. It is faced with Irish limestone and inside the floors are of reinforced concrete.

Stephen Gwynn wrote that *"The architect has shown something approaching genius in the conversion of an old exhibition building into a very noble building . . . simple, severe and most dignified."*

END PAVILION, UNIVERSITY COLLEGE, EARLSFORT TERRACE.

architect served articles under the established practitioner. As long as traditional methods of building continued in use, this knowledge could be passed on from master to pupil, but more novel approaches to design and onstruction gave rise to demands for more up to date instruction. These were partially met by classes and lectures organised from time to time by the Architectural Association of Ireland (founded 1871, revived 1896) while excursions and sketching tours helped architects to study important buildings both at home and abroad. The establishment of regular and part-time courses of study for architects did not come about until much later. Although such courses commenced in England in the nineties, academic training for Irish architects began only when the National University of Ireland was founded in 1908.

Early in the 19th century a growing awareness of the role of the architect led to the formation in 1839 of the Royal Institute of the Architects of Ireland. The first vice-President (1839-44) was Sir Richard Morrison. The President was Lord Fitzgerald and de Vesci who acted as patron. The custom of appointing a nobleman as President was abandoned in 1863 when Sir Charles Lanyon was elected to the office. By this time the membership of the Institute included practically all the prominent figures who, as professional men, accepted a code of practice (which included a scale of fees) as a guide to their relationship with clients and builders. Far-reaching changes were also taking place in the building industry. The master craftsman was being replaced by the general contractor employing others to do the work. The type of client was also changing from the patron to the businessman (or committee), who unlike his 18th century predecessor, was generally without any knowledge of architectural style.

The development of competitive "lump sum" tendering followed the rise of the general contractor. This called for more elaborate and detailed drawings and a more comprehensive specification of materials describing how they were to be used and laid. These, in turn, led to the preparation of "bills of quantities" relating to both materials and workmanship. Initially, architects prepared their own "bills" but the emergence of the quanity surveyor came about as a necessary part of the building industry. Mechanisation in some trades gradually replaced hand work. The use of precast plaster work in which ornament could be bought by the gross, was an example of the changing processes in building, apart from those brought about by new and novel materials. Greater demands than, perhaps, ever before, were made upon the architect. He had to be familiar with various styles of architecture, to devise plans for new types of buildings and to conform to legislation and bye-laws affecting his work. This growing complexity of practice was reflected in designs carried out in a variety of fashions as each was, in its time and place, regarded as the only true and appropriate style of the day.

In the nineteenth century the role of the architect got royal recognition by the bestowal of knighthoods on no less than five members of the profession who carried out work in Dublin. These were Sir Thomas Deane (1830); Sir Richard Morrison (1883); Sir Thomas Drew (1900). The last Irish architect to be honoured was

MUSUEM, NOW SCHOOL OF ENGIN- EERING, TRINITY COLLEGE.

Other picutres of buildings in Trinity College are on pages 135-139

The Museum (now the School of Engineering), Trinity College, was designed in the Lombardic Venetian style by Deane and Woodward and completed in 1857. Carvings were executed by the O'Shea brothers, James and John. Inside, the decoration is polychromatic.

Other buildings designed by Benjamin Woodward include the Kildare Street Club. He was also responsible for the barrel vault in the Trinity College Library erected in 1859.

The red brick building known as the Rubrics was completed in the early part of the Eighteenth Century but the top storey was altered in 1891.

RUBRICS, TRINITY COLLEGE.

Sir T Manly Deane (1911), a son of Sir T Newenham Deane and grandson of Sir Thomas Deane.

GOVERNMENT
BUILDINGS,
UPPER MERRION
STREET.

*Leinster Lawn
is on the right.
Pictures of Leinster
House are on page
94.*

The Government Buildings in Upper Merrion Street were designed by Sir Aston Webb and Thomas Manly Deane in a very heavy Neo-Classical style foreign to Dublin. The first stage was completed in 1911, with further additions in 1922 and later.

*The entrance to the
College of Science is in
the centre of the build-
ing. Pictures of the
College of Science on
page 74 and page 96.*

GOVERNMENT
BUILDINGS,
UPPER MERRION
STREET.

COLLEGE OF SCIENCE AS SEEN THROUGH GATEWAY IN SCREEN COLONNADE

A monumental colonnade screens the courtyard in front of the College of Science in Upper Merrion Street. Although an impressive feature of the complex the detail is rather coarse. Designed by Aston Webb of London, with local supervision by Thomas Manly Deane, the college was completed in 1911.

The College of Science was originally located in St. Stephen's Green, in premises now occupied by the Office of Public Works.

The Fusiliers' Arch, St. Stephen's Green, was completed in 1907 as a Boer War memorial. John Howard Pentland, together with Sir Thomas Drew as consultant, were responsible for the design.

The other gates and piers of St. Stephen's Green were designed by J. F. Fuller.

MEMORIAL
GATEWAY,
ST. STEPHEN'S GREEN.

THE FIRST QUARTER OF THE TWENTIETH CENTURY

The early part of the twentieth century was a period of comparative unrest in the building industry. Few new churches were required following the building activites of the latter half of the nineteenth century. New public buildings were rare. Only two of outstanding importance were undertaken in Dublin before the outbreak of World War I. The first, the College of Science and Government Buildings in Upper Merrion Street, was designed by Sir Aston Webb of London in a heavy and massive Renaissance style. Grouping the buildings around a forecourt, separated from the street by a colonnade screen, was a fine conception, but the overall effect is marred by the coarseness of the detail. Sir T M Deane, who was associated with Webb as a joint architect, appears to have had little influence over the design, which owes nothing to the classical traditions of the city.

The second was the new University College, Earlsfort Terrace. The Dublin architect, R M Butler, later to become Professor of Architecture in UCD, was commissioned to design the building as a result of a public competition held in 1912. The assessor was Henry H Hare, a well-known English architect of the period. The College building is designed in the Greek Revival style. The main facade is composed of a colonnaded entrance, flanking wings and end pavilions recalling the riverside elevation of Gandon's Custom House. As an example of neo-classical architecture it is a worthy if austere design. Unfortunately, the Irish limestone used in its construction has not weathered or mellowed sufficiently to soften the unsympathetic effect of this hard material compared with Portland stone. As costs increased during the war the building grant was insufficient to complete the scheme, so that when the College was opened in 1918 the old Exhibition Buildings of 1865, still standing on the site, had to be utilised for staff and student accommodation. Some parts of these old buildings are still used for this purpose but the Great Hall has been restored to its original use and is now An Ceoláras Náisiúnta/The National Concert Hall. The choice of the Classical style, rather than the Medieval style, for the UCD building, as well as for the North British Assurance Building, now No. 1 Dawson Street, designed by Dick Peddie and Washington Browne of Edinburgh about the same time, was mainly as a result of an academic reaction which followed the Gothic Revival style.

Although the Gothic style still prevailed for church building, not all churches were built in that manner. St Agatha's, North William Street (off the North Strand) was designed in the Roman Renaissance style by William H Byrne of Dublin. It is an imposing example of an aisleless nave of great height ending in a spacious semi-circular apse forming the sanctuary, a plan very different in spatial values from the nave and aisles of the typical Gothic church. Massively built of stone, it withstood without a shake the German air raid on the North Strand in 1941.

Stone as well as brick was still reasonably economic as a building material, even for smaller works. Native granite and limestone provided good building stones, but

ROYAL
VICTORIA
EYE AND
EAR
HOSPITAL,
ADELAIDE
ROAD.

The location of the National Eye and Ear Hospital, founded in 1801, was changed several times and eventually it was opened as the Royal Victoria Eye and Ear Hospital in Adelaide Road in 1904. The red brick Renaissance style building, designed by Rawson Carroll and Fred Bachelor, has many attractive features.

Mercer's Hospital, founded in 1734 by Mrs. Mary Mercer, has closed down but the hospital building, which had already been altered and extended over the years, has been adapted to provide accommodation for students and staff of the Royal College of Surgeons.

MERCER'S
HOSPITAL,
STEPHEN'S
STREET.

tended to become dull and grey in an increasingly polluted city atmosphere. In 1913 Pearse Street Gárda Station building was designed by Andrew Robinson of the Board of Works for the police of the time. The facade of County Dublin granite is now dull by comparison with the clean and sparkling appearance of the same material used by the architect W H Byrne in the Christian Brothers' Novitiate, Marino. Brick was more resistant to pollution, as evidenced in the well-preserved facade of Royal Victoria Eye and Ear Hospital, Adelaide Road, designed by Rawson Carroll and Bachelor (c.1901) in a French Renaissance style

Apart from utilitarian structures, concrete was little used at this time for buildings, and there are certainly very few examples where it was exposed externally. The Land Registry, Chancery Street (c.1914) has external facings partly of concrete bricks and blocks with granite steps and entrance. The architect was J H Pentland of the Office of Public Works. For larger buildings architects could no longer ignore the practical advantages and economy of both steel and concrete. Easons of O'Connell Street has a reinforced concrete frame with stone facings to the facades, designed by the English architect J H Rutven. Clery's Department Store, on the opposite side of the street, has a steel frame with stonework attached to the steel. It was designed by Ashlin and Coleman of Dublin. Both of these buildings were built as part of the reconstruction after the 1916 Rising.

Although the prevailing style was Classical, architects sometimes tried to match the purpose or importance of the building with an appropriate external expression, which sometimes had little relationship to the form of construction. These modes or styles ranged from the Roman Classical used by Pentland for the Memorial Arch, St Stephen's Green, though variations of Medieval and Renaissance architecture down to a type of English vernacular popularised by Norman Shaw and others. Their influence may be seen in the gate lodge, St Stephen's Green, and later in Dawson Chambers, Dawson Street, particularly in the use and treatment of oriel windows. The Art Noveau style which originated on the European Continent and sought inspiration from nature, had little or no influence in this country. There are only a few isolated examples of the style in Dublin. The Celtic literary and dramatic movements of the day left architecture largely untouched except for the short-lived revival of the Irish Romanesque style. In the Church of St Columba (1904) the architects, Ashlin and Coleman, adapted ornament and decoration from native sources to an otherwise ordinary Medieval design. It is located at Iona Road.

In the subsidiary arts associated with church design such as stained glass, textiles, embroidery and enamel work, great progress was made. A fine school of stained glass artists flourished and examples of their work may be found far beyond their native shores. An interest in the Georgian architecture of the capital began to arouse scholarly attention, and resulted in the founding of the Georgian Society and the publication of the splendid volumes on the work of this special phase. Another event arising out of an even wider interest in the city and its development was the competition in 1914 for a physical plan for Dublin, which was won by Abercrombie and Kelly of Liverpool. Their layout was based on Classical principles of planning so

O'CONNELL BRIDGE AND O'CONNELL STREET.

Most of the buildings in O'Connell Street were either destroyed or badly damaged during the Rising in 1916 and much discussion about the architectural possibilities of reconstruction soon followed. A plea by the architect William A. Scott for a unified scheme was rejected and the property owners each had individual designs drawn up for their buildings. In general the reconstruction was disappointing from an architectural point of view and subsequent developments have not improved the appearance of the capital's main street. On the contrary, new shop fronts and a plethora of garish advertising signs and fascias has done much to impair the architectural features of the streetscape.

Other monuments and statues are illustrated on pages 156-159.

The O'Connell Monument, by John Henry Foley, was unveiled in 1882. Below the statue of the Liberator, Éire and other representative figures are ranged around a cylindrical column. Below them, facing in four different directions, are statues of winged Victories representing Patriotism, Fidelity, Eloquence and Courage.

O'CONNELL MONUMENT, O'CONNELL STREET.

as to permit, mainly through street improvements, visual features such as long straight thoroughfares with their related buildings and vistas on the lines of Hausmann's Paris. World War I and the Irish War of Independence caused the postponement of the competition proposals which, in time, became outmoded and were finally abandoned.

The 1916 Rising resulted in the destruction of a considerable amount of property including the major part of O'Connell Street, which was, up to then, a fine example of a Georgian street. There was a considerable amount of discussion amongst architects and others as to how best the street should be reconstructed. R M Butler, referring to 'the wonderful and unlooked-for opportunity' which had arisen, was not short of suggestions as to the new buildings which might be located in the street — a Gallery of Modern Art to house Sir Hugh Lane's paintings; a new home for the Royal Hibernian Academy; a school for progressive Irish art; a National Theatre; a hall with an organ worthy of the capital; new offices for the Bank of Ireland, or a new Parliament House, as the case might be. These public buildings would, according to his suggestions, form the salient features of a noble thoroughfare. He went further, saying "The possibilities are infinite; for the reconstruction of the street might form the nucleus of a great scheme, the creation of magnificent riverside frontages, both sides of the Liffey from the Custom House to Kingsbridge". He realised, of course, that to carry out such schemes state aid and ample statutory powers would be necessary, and his prophecy that these would not be provided by the British Government proved true. He had put forward a less ambitious contingency plan involving a coordinated treatment for the street frontages using native materials. In the event his plea for a unified approach to design of the facades was not heeded, and he considered the eventual reconstruction as an architectural disaster. The Committee of the Dublin Fire and Property Losses Association had threatened strong opposition to any scheme: 1. which delays building operations; 2. which imposes architectural features which are not in harmony with the needs of each individual trader; 3. which puts extra expenses on property owners or alters existing frontage lines without full compensation. W A Scott, on behalf of the citizens (whom, he pointed out, contributed not a little to the value of the property involved), firmly demanded that the interests of private individuals should not override the wider interests of the community and art. He sought to allay the fears of the property owners, explaining that an organic scheme or unified plan need not mean a spiritless uniformity, but a general scheme of mass-grouping, unity amid variety, a balance of manner and proportions. W A Scott called for concerted action amongst architects and offered the services of the Royal Institute of the Architects of Ireland towards this end. But this was of no avail. The rebuilding of the devastated areas was, unfortunately, a lost opportunity mainly through a failure to adopt some unifying discipline in order to achieve a fine architectural effect. The street as rebuilt is, however, saved from banality by the General Post Office, restored in 1926, which still dominates the scene.

The electric tramways which first came into operation in 1896, gave an impetus to suburban developments, particularly to those building, in areas between the city

VIEW
OF
CITY
FROM
RANELAGH,
LOOKING
SOUTH.

For the most part the older areas of the city consist of low-rise buildings, few more than four storeys in height. Here and there the skyline is broken by some important public building rising above the general level of its surroundings. From Ranelagh, looking south towards the mountains, the Church of Our Lady of Refuge, Rathmines, and the Town Hall, Rathmines, punctuate the scene. The area view here was rapidly developed in the Nineteenth Century.

From Parnell Square, again looking south, the Four Courts, the cathedrals and other churches can be identified, while the Dublin mountains provide an attractive backdrop.

VIEW OF
CITY
FROM
PARNELL
SQUARE.

80

proper and the older communities, some of which were grouped near the outer railway stations. Hitherto the suburbs had been the privilege of the wealthy merchants and shopkeepers, but smaller houses and a cheap and frequent transport service began to entice the middle classes away from the closely packed city streets to the more appealing environments close to sea and countryside. To this period, which lasted up to the outbreak of World War II, belongs the development of Drumcondra and the north suburbs in general, as well as areas adjacent to the Circular Roads, part of Donnybrook, Ranelagh, etc. Most of the houses, however comfortable, had little architectural merit. Exceptions were, however, some building estates outside the city at Foxrock and Greystones. These were developed with greater attention to architectural design. The architects chiefly involved were Sir T M Deane, Richard Caulfield Orpen and Fred Batchelor. After World War II and the gradual resumption of building activity, the bungalow became popular as a dwelling unit. In general, significant progresss in housing and slum clearance was not made until some years after the establishment of the Irish Free State.

HOUSES,
TERENURE.

Other houses are illustrated on pages 184-197.

This terrace of houses, with its polygonal masonry and decorative details around windows and doors, is in strong contrast to the more conventional simple and straightforward treatment of the detached house shown below.

Decorative brick and stone facades, similar to those shown above, may also be seen on Northumberland Road and elsewhere in the southern suburbs.

LIFFEY BRIDGES

South of River		North of River
HEUSTON STATION	SARAH BRIDGE 1791	CONYNGHAM ROAD
STEEVEN'S LANE	**KING'S BRIDGE 1828** Renamed	PARKGATE STREET
VICTORIA QUAY	SEÁN HEUSTON BRIDGE	WOLFE TONE QUAY
GUINNESS'S BREWERY		
	FRANK SHERWIN BRIDGE 1982	
WATLING STREET	**VICTORIA BRIDGE 1863** Renamed	ELLIS QUAY · COLLINS' BARRACKS
USHER'S QUAY	RORY O'MORE BRIDGE	
BRIDGEFOOT ST.	QUEEN'S BRIDGE Rebuilt 1768	QUEEN'S STREET
USHER'S QUAY	Renamed LIAM MELLOWS' BRIDGE 1942	ARRAN QUAY · ST. PAUL'S CHURCH
BRIDGE STREET	**WHITWORTH BRIDGE 1813** New balustrade	CHURCH STREET
ADAM & EVE'S	1890	
MERCHANT'S QUAY	Renamed FR. MATHEW BRIDGE 1938	INNS QUAY · FOUR COURTS
WINETAVERN STREET	**RICHMOND BRIDGE 1813** Replaced	CHANCERY PLACE
ST. MICHAEL & JOHN'S CHURCH · WOOD QUAY	ORMOND BRIDGE Renamed O'DONOVAN ROSSA BRIDGE	ORMOND QUAY
ESSEX QUAY PARLIAMENT ST.	**ESSEX BRIDGE Rebuilt 1875** Renamed	CAPEL STREET
WELLINGTON QUAY	GRATTAN BRIDGE **WELLINGTON BRIDGE,** LIFFEY BRIDGE, METAL BRIDGE or HA'PENNY BRIDGE **1816**	ORMOND QUAY · LIFFEY STREET
ASTON QUAY	CARLISLE BRIDGE 1794 Rebuilt and Renamed **O'CONNELL BRIDGE 1880**	BACHELOR'S WALK
BURGH QUAY TARA STREET GEORGE'S QUAY CITY QUAY	**BUTT BRIDGE 1879** Rebuilt 1932	EDEN QUAY · CUSTOM HOUSE QUAY · CUSTOM HOUSE
	LOOP LINE RAILWAY BRIDGE 1891	
MOSS STREET	MATT TABLOT MEMORIAL BRIDGE 1978	AMIENS STREET
SIR JOHN ROGERSON'S QUAY		
	EAST LINK BRIDGE 1985	*Names and dates of the bridges built in the 19th Century are in bold type.*

BIBLIOGRAPHY

General

Ball, F.E.   An historical sketch of the Pembroke Township. The vicinity of the International Exhibition, Dublin. Alex Thom 1907. Carraig Books Reprints, Dublin. 1983.

Bielenberg, C.   A guided tour of Dublin. Illustrated by Robert Pim. The Mercier Press, Cork.

Bolger, W. and Share, B.   And Nelson on his pillar. 1806-1966. Nonpareil Press, Dublin. 1976.

Butler, R.M.   Irish architecture. Saorstát Éireann Handbook Dublin. 1932. pp. 7-8.

Cook, J.M.   Victorian architecture. A visual anthology Johnston Reprint Company, London. 1971. pp. 8, 92 128, 254.

Cosgrave, D.   North Dublin city and environs. Catholic Truth Society, Dublin. 1909. Reprinted by Four Courts Press, Dublin, 1979.

Craig, M.   Architecture in Ireland. Department of External Affairs, Dublin. 1978. pp.49-52.

Craig, M.   Dublin 1660-1860. Allen Figgis, Dublin. 1969. pp. 278-381.

Craig, M. and Knight of Glin   Ireland observed. Cork Examiner/Mercier Press. 1970. pp.48-50.

Craig, M.   The architecture of Ireland from earliest times to 1880. Batsford, London and Eason, Dublin. 1982.

Curriculum Development Unit   Dublin 1913. A divided city. The O'Brien Press, Dublin. 1982.

de Breffney, B. and ffolliott, R.   The houses of Ireland. Photographed by George Mott. Thames and Hudson, London. 1983.

Dalton J.   History of County Dublin. Hodges and Smith. 1838. Reprinted by Tower Books, Cork, 1976.

Daly, M.E.   Dublin — The deposed capital; a social and economic history, 1860-1914. Cork University Press.

Dickenson, P.L.   The Dublin of yesterday. Methuen, London. 1929.

Dublin Arts Festival   Programme of the Dublin Arts Festival, Dublin. 1973.

Dunne, J.J.   Streets broad and narrow. A personal view of Dublin. Helicon, Dublin. 1982.

CUSTOM
HOUSE

*The building of
the North Wall
and the East Wall
was started in
1717 and finished
in 1728.*

*The North
Bull Wall
was built
about 1825.*

*Following the building of the Custom House wharves and warehouses were built on the North Wall
and Sheriff Street, Mayor Street, Guild Street and Commons Street were developed.*

The Custom House, designed by James Gandon, was commenced in 1781 and completed in 1791. After a fire in 1833 it was reconstructed with major alterations. It was burned in 1921 and subsequently rebuilt in 1927-29 and has recently been renovated. The statue of Hope on top of the copper covered dome is over 38 m above street level.

James Gandon, born in London in 1743, died in Lucan in 1823 and is buried with the antiquarian, Francis Grose, in the cemetery attached to the Church of St. John the Baptist, Drumcondra.

St. Columba's Church, designed by Ashlin and Coleman, was built in 1906.

The new Catholic parish of Drumcondra was formed in 1902. A small wooden-framed church was in use in Glasnevin until the present one was built in 1970.

GANDON'S TOMB,
DRUMCONDRA.

Bibliography

Dunphy, Austin	An outline history of Dublin. RIBA Conference Programme, London. 1966.
Ferguson, S.	Architecture in Ireland. University Magazine, Dublin. 1847. Vol. 29, pp. 695-708.
Fitzpatrick, S.A.O.	Dublin: Historical and typographical account of the city. Illustrated by W. Curtis Green. First published by Methuen, London. 1907. Tower Books, Cork. 1977.
Georgian Society	Georgian Society Records. Dublin. 1909. 13 vols.
Gilbert, J.T.	A history of the city of Dublin. 3 vols. James McGlashan, 1854-59. Facsimile reprint. Irish University Press, Shannon. 1972. Gill and MacMillan, Dublin. 1978.
Glin, Knight of	Malton's Dublin, 1799. A picturesque and descriptive view of the city of Dublin. Reproduced from the original, with introduction by the Knight of Glin. Dolmen Press, Dublin. 1978.
Gorham, M.	Dublin old and new. E.P. Publications, Wakefield, England. 1975.
Guinness, D.	Portrait of Dublin. B.T. Batsford, London. 1967.
Harbison, P.	Irish art and architecture from prehistory to the present. Thames and Hudson, London. 1978.
Harvey, J.	Dublin. A study in environment. Batsford London. 1949. Reprinted with new introduction and postscript by the author. S.R. Publications, Wakefield, England. 1972.
Hickey, D.J. and Doherty, J.E.	A dictionary of Irish history since 1800. Gill and MacMillan, Dublin.
Hughes, N.J.	Irish engineering, 1760-1960. The institution of Engineers of Ireland, Dublin. 1982.
Hutchins, P.	James Joyce's Dublin. The Grey Walls Press. 1950.
Joyce, W. St. J.	The neighbourhood of Dublin: it's typography antiquities and historical associations. M.H. Gill, Dublin. 1939. Republished by S.R. Publications, Wakefield, England. 1971. Gill and MacMillan, London. 1976.
Judge, P.W. (Ed)	O'Connell School. 150 years, 1828-1978. Dublin. 1978.
Kain, R.M.	Dublin in the age of William Butler Yeats and James Joyce. David and Charles, Newton Abbot. 1972.
Kearns, K.C.	Georgian Dublin. Ireland's imperilled architectural heritage. David and Charles, London. 1983.

GENERAL POST OFFICE, LOWER O'CONNELL STREET.

The General Post Office was designed by Francis Johnston and built in 1814-18. Many alterations were carried out to the building in the latter half of the Nineteenth Century. Further alterations and extensions were carried out in the period 1904-15. It was damaged in 1916 but subsequently reconstructed, the granite facade (68 m wide and 15 m high) being preserved. The hexastyle Ionic portico is built of Portland stone. Standing above the pediment are statues of Hibernia, Mercury and Fidelity.

Other buildings in O'Connell Street, damaged in 1916, were reconstructed in the mid-twenties. Clery's department store, opposite the GPO, was designed by Ashlin and Coleman. The foundation stone of that building was laid in 1920.

The central part of the Parliament House in College Green, designed by Edward Lovett Pearce, was built in 1729. Subsequently alterations were carried out under the direction of James Gandon, Edward Parke and others. When the building was taken over by the Bank of Ireland it was adapted by Francis Johnston to meet the requirements of the new owner. This work was carried out between 1803 and 1808. The House of Lord's portico and the eastern extension, designed by James Gandon, was finished in 1789.

HOUSE OF LORDS' PORTICO,
BANK OF IRELAND,
WESTMORELAND STREET.

Bibliography

Kelly, D.	Hands off Dublin. O'Brien Press, Dublin. 1976.
Kennedy, T. (Ed)	Victorian Dublin. Albertine Kennedy Publishing, Dublin. 1980.
Lalor, B.	Dublin. Ninety drawings. Routledge and Keegan Paul, London. 1981.
Lehane, B.	The great cities — Dublin. With photographs by John McDermott and Laurie Lee. Time-Life Books, Amsterdam.
Little, F.J.	A glimpse of Victorian Dublin. Dublin Historical Record. 1943. Vol. 6, No. 1. pp. 8-24.
McDermott, M.J.	Ireland's architectural heritage. Edited and illustrated by A. Brioscú. Folens, Dublin. 1975.
McDonagh, O.	Ireland. The Union and its aftermath. George Allen and Unwin, London, 1977.
MacGiolla Phádraig, B.	History of Terenure. Veritas Company Ltd. Dublin. 1954.
MacLoughlin	A Guide to historic Dublin. Gill and MacMillan, Dublin. 1979.
McPartland, E.	The Wide Streets Commissioners: their importance for Dublin architecture in the eighteenth century and early nineteenth century. Irish Georgian Society Quarterly Bulletin. 1972. Vol. 15, January to March.
Magowan, R.S.	Dublin and Cork. Photographs introduced by Kate O'Brien. Spring Books, London. 1961.
Malone, J.B. and Martin, L.C.	Know your Dublin. Scepter Books, Dublin. 1969.
Maxwell, C.	Dublin under the Georges 1714-1830. Faber and Faber, London. 1956.
Mitchell, F.H.	Vanishing Dublin. Allen Figgis, Dublin. 1966.
Moore, D.F.	Dublin. Cultural Relations Committee, Dublin. 1965.
Morrison, G.	An Irish Camera. Pan Books, London. 1979.
Muthesius, S.	The high Victorian movement in architecture. Routledge and Keegan Paul, London. 1972.
National Gallery of Ireland	The architecture of Ireland in drawings and paintings. Exhibition catalogue. 1975.
Nolan, J.	Changing faces. St. Vincent's Tontine and Burial Society, Dublin. 1982.

The first stone of the Fourt Courts was laid in 1786 and the building was finished in 1803. Thomas Cooley was the architect originally commissioned but James Gandon was later put in charge. The building was badly damaged in the Civil War in 1922 but it was subsequently reconstructed with significant alterations. The work was completed in 1932.

There are some interesting buildings behind the Four Courts. The Land Registry, designed by John Howard Pentland, was built in 1914. The classical Public Records Office and Record Repository was built in 1864-67 and the Bridewell was built in 1866-68.

The Hospital of King Charles or Blue Coat School was founded in 1669 as a hospital for the aged and free school for poor children. The original building was replaced in 1773-80 by one designed by Thomas Ivory who also laid out the adjoining street. The copper covered cupola, now a prominent feature of the building, was erected in 1894. Curved wings and end pavilions face onto the attractive forecourt. The building was carefully restored for the Incorporated Law Society who own the building since 1979.

INCORPORATED
LAW SOCIETY
BUILDING,
FORMERLY
KING'S
HOSPITAL
SCHOOL
OR
BLUECOAT
SCHOOL,
BLACKHALL
PLACE.

O'Connor, L.	Lost Ireland. Photographic record at the turn of the 19th century with an introduction and commentary by Patrick Gallagher. Rainbow Publications Ltd., Dublin. 1984.
O'Connell, D.	The antique pavement. An Taisce, Dublin. 1975.
O'Dwyer, F.	Lost Dublin. Gill and MacMillan, Dublin. 1981.
O'Flaherty, G.	Dublin. Illustrations by Peter Jay. No. 37 of the Irish Environmental Series. Folens, Dublin.
Ó'Súilleabháin	Ó Kingstown go Dún Laoghaire. Foilseacháin Náisiúnta Teoranta. Baile Átha Cliath. 1976.
Pearson, P.	Dún Laoghaire: Kingstown. O'Brien Press, Dublin. 1981.
Piatt, D.	Cois Life fadó. Foilseacháin Náisiúnta Teoranta. Baile Átha Cliath. 1985.
Piatt, D.	Mhaireadar san Ardchathair. FAS, Baile Átha Cliath. 1957.
Plunkett, J.	Dublin. Photographs by Ian Finlay and Mike Bunn. Introduction by James Plunkett. Dublin Corporation. 1976.
Prichett, V.S.	Dublin, a portrait. Photographs by E. Hofer. The Bodley Head, London. 1967.
Robertson, Manning	Cautionary guide to Dublin. Royal Institute of the Architects of Ireland, Dublin.
Somerville Large, P.	Dublin. Hamish Hamilton, London. 1979. Granada, London. 1981.
Taisce, An	'Urbanana' Dublin's List I buildings. A conservation report for An Taisce, sponsored by the Heritage Trust. 1982.
Viney, M.	Victorian Ireland. The Irish Times, Dublin. January 24, 1975. p. 10.
Wright, G.N.	An historical guide to the city of Dublin. Illustrated by engravings and a plan of the city. Baldwin, Craddock and Joy, London. 1825. Reprint by Four Courts Press and Irish Academic Press, Dublin. 1980.

ARCHITECTS

Betjeman, J.	Francis Johnston, Irish architect. The Pavilion, I.T. Publications, London. 1946.

WEST
FRONT,
KING'S
INNS,
FACING
CONSTITUTION
HILL.

The building of the King's Inns was commenced in 1795, opened in 1798 and completed about 1817. It was designed by James Gandon and finished by his pupil Henry Aaron Baker, with later additions by Francis Johnston. The wings were added in the early Nineteenth Century.

The Library in Henrietta Street, designed by Frederick Darley, was built in 1827. Jacob Owen designed the Registry of Deeds built in 1849.

Interesting features of the west front of the King's Inns are the caryatids and the bas-relief panels. On the other side of the building there is a monumental entrance gateway at the end of Henrietta Street, leading into an enclosed court with the Bencher's Hall on one side. The cupola adds interest to the skyline.

The park, an amenity enjoyed by the local community, has a fine masonry wall built in the Nineteenth Century.

THE
KING'S
INNS.

Bibliography

Curran, C.P.	Benjamin Woodward, architect: his work in Ireland and England. 1940. Vol. 29, p. 229.
McDermott, M.J.	The Byrnes RIAI Yearbook 1980. RIAI, Dublin. 1980. The Darleys RIAI Yearbook 1981. RIAI, Dublin. 1981. The Deans RIAI Yearbook 75/76. RIAI, Dublin. 1976. The Morrisons RIAI Yearbook 1977. RIAI, Dublin. 1977. The Murrays RIAI Yearbook 1979. RIAI, Dublin. 1979.
McParland, E.	Francis Johnston 1760-1829. Irish Georgian Society Quarterly Bulletin, Dublin. Vol. 7, April to December 1964. pp. 48-67.
O'Dwyer, F.	Benjamin Woodward. The Pre-Raphaelite architect. Boethius Press, Co. Kilkenny. 1985.
Ware, D.	A short history of British architecture. Allen and Unwin, London. 1967.

BUILDINGS

Finlay, I. and Bunn, M.	Photographs of Dublin with an introduction by J. Plunkett. Dublin Corporation. 1976.
Hemp, W.	If ever you go to Dublin town. Devin-Adair, Old Grenwich, England. 1979.
Malton, J.	A picturesque and descriptive view of the city. Reproduced from the 1799 edition with an introduction by the Knight of Glin. Dolmen Press and Georgian Society, Dublin. 1978.
Tyrell, G. and Craig, M.	Views of Dublin. Dublin delineated in views of the principal public buildings. Printed for G. Tyrell, 1837. Facsimile reprint with new introduction by M. Craig. S.R. Publishers, Wakefield, England. 1971.

Halls, Club, Theatre

Jones, A.G.	Dublin exhibition palace and winter garden. Dublin Builder. 1864. Vol. 6, No. 101, March 1, pp. 36, 39.
	Theatre in South King Street. Irish Builder. 1871. Vol. 13, No. 27, July 15. pp. 188-9.
	Merrion Hall, Dublin Builder. 1863. Vol. 5, No. 89, September 1, pp. 145-146.
	Kildare Street Club. Dublin Builder. 1860. Vol. 2, No. 19, July. pp. 292-3.

Iveagh House

Sheaf, N.	Iveagh House. An historical description. Department of Foreign Affairs, Dublin 1978.

IVEAGH PLAY CENTRE, BULL ALLEY.

The Iveagh Play Centre, designed by McDonnell and Reid, architects, and built by the Trust in 1913, has an imposing symmetrical facade facing St. Patrick's Park. The accommodation includes spacious classrooms and a hall. These are now used by the Liberties Vocational School.

The Iveagh Trust was also responsible for the development of St. Patrick's Park after the clearance of the slums which had occupied the site.

ST. PATRICK'S CATHEDRAL.

WAY DETAIL.

Bibliography

Jail

Stephenson, P.J.   Kilmainham Jail. Dublin Historical Record. 1955. Vol. 14, No. 3. p. 65.

*Leinster House,
Gallery Library,
Museum*

Tóibin, S.   Teach Laighean. Suíomh Dháil Éireann agus Seanad Éireann. Oifig an tSoláthair, Baile Átha Cliath. 1975.

National Gallery of Ireland. Dublin Builder. 1888. Vol. 8, No. 18, August 15. pp. 206-7.

National Library of Ireland. Irish Builder, Dublin. 1884. Vol. 26, No. 296, October 15, p. 302.

A bird's eye view of the new National Library and Museum, Kildare Street. Irish Builder, Dublin. 1803. Vol. 35, No. 797, March 5. pp 54-55, 61.

Science and Art 1877-1977. Catalogue of exhibition featuring the National Library and the National Museum. 1977.

Banks and Offices

Crown Life Building, Dame Street. T.N. Deane, architect. Irish Builder, Dublin. 1871. Vol. 13, No. 273, May 1. pp. 112-113.

Hibernian Bank, College Green. W.G. Murray, architect. 1862. Irish Builder, Dublin. Vol. 5, No. 96, December 15. p. 201.

Northern Assurance Company, 7 Westmoreland Street. G.C. Ashlin, architect. Irish Builder, Dublin. 1886. Vol. 28, No. 641, September 1. p. 251.

Northern Banking Co. Ltd. Grafton Street. W.H. Lynn. Irish Builder. 1903. Vol. 44, No. 1044, May 21.

Royal Insurance Building. Irish Builder, Dublin, 1869. Vol. 11, No. 227, June 1. p. 128.

Sun Life and Fire Office, St. Andrew's Street, G.C. Ashlin, architect. Irish Builder, Dublin. Vol. 28, No. 635, pp. 161, 165.

Ulster Bank, College Green. T. Drew, architect. Irish Builder, Dublin. 1891. January 15. pp. 18-19.

Castles

Caisleán Bhaile Átha Cliath. Cúlra staire agus eolaí. Dublin Castle.

WEST
FRONT,
LEINSTER
HOUSE,
FACING
KILDARE
STREET.

WEST FRONT OF LEINSTER HOUSE, FACING KILDARE STREET.

Leinster House was bought by the Dublin Society from the Duke of Leinster in 1815. The entrance gateway in Kildare Street dates from the beginning of the Twentieth Century. The original house was designed by Richard Cassels and built in 1745. After the Royal Dublin Society (as it was titled from 1820) moved to Ballsbridge in 1921 the building was converted for use as the meeting place of the Oireachtas. It has been used for this purpose since 1922 but the original conversion was not completed until 1926 and further alterations have been carried out since then.

EAST FRONT OF LEINSTER HOUSE, FACING LAWN AND MERRION SQUARE.

EAST
FRONT,
LEINSTER
HOUSE,
FACING
LEINSTER
LAWN
AND
MERRION
SQUARE.

Bibliography

Historical background and guide. Stationery Office, Dublin for the Commissioners of Public Works.

de Breffny, B.   Castles of Ireland. Photographs by George Mott. Thames and Hudson, London. 1977.

Churches

Brioscú, A.   Irish churches. Environmental Series. Folens, Dublin. 1967.

Carey, F.P.   Catholic Dublin. A guide to all the principal churches. Trinity Press, Dublin. 1932.

de Breffny, B. and Mott, G.   Churches and abbeys of Ireland. Thames and Hudson, London. 1976. pp. 142-179.

Donnelly, N.   Short histories of Dublin parishes. Carraig Chapbooks, Dublin.

Jackson, V.   St. Patrick's Cathedral. Irish Heritage Series, Eason, Dublin. 1976.

Kennedy, T.P.   Church building. A history of Irish Catholicism Vol. 5, Chapter 8. Gill and MacMillan, Dublin. 1970.

Kerr, R.J.   The Parish and church of St. George, Dublin. Second Impression, Dublin. 1967.

Pontz, S.G.   St. Ann's. The church in the heart of the city 1976.

Purcell, M.   Dublin's Pro-Cathedral 1825-1975. Published at the Pro-Cathedral Dublin. 1975.

Sheehy, J.   J.J. McCarthy and the Gothic revival in Ireland. Ulster Architectural and Historical Society. 1977.

Stokes, A.E.   Christ Church Cathedral. Irish Heritage Series, Eason, Dublin. 1978.

Wheeler, H.A.   The Dublin city churches of the Church of Ireland. APCK, Dublin. 1948.

Commercial and Industrial Buildings

Oram, H.   Bewley's Dublin. Albertine Kennedy, Dublin. 1980.

Arnott and Co. New premises. G.P. Sleator, architect. Irish Builder, Dublin. 1895. Vol. 37, No. 847, April. pp. 83, 88-89.

Cabinet warehouses, Stafford Street. W.G. Murray, architect. Dublin Builder. 1865. Vol. 7, No. 121, February 15. pp. 48-49.

NATIONAL
GALLERY
OF IRELAND,
MERRION
SQUARE.

The National Gallery of Ireland, Merrion Square, was first opened in 1864. Designed by Francis Fowke and Sir Richard Griffith, it was later enlarged to the design of Sir Thomas Deane. The portico of Ballybrew granite and Portland stone, featuring rusticated columns, was added in 1903. The gallery was more recently extended again by the Office of Public Works.

In front of the building is a statue of William Dargan, benefactor of the Dublin Exhibition of 1853.

The Renaissance style College of Science, designed by Sir Aston Webb and Thomas Manly Deane, was built in 1911. The Royal College of Science was transferred to University College Dublin in 1926.

COLLEGE
OF
SCIENCE,
UPPER
MERRION
STREET.

96

Bibliography

Guinness's Brewery. From the Brewer's Journal. Dublin Builder. 1865. Vol. 7, No. 137, September 1. p. 216.

J.G. Mooney's new premises, Sackville Street and Abbey Street. J.N. Deane, architect. Irish Builder, Dublin. 1872. pp. 253-259.

Messers W. Smyth & Sons' new buildings. A.G. Jones, architect. Irish Builder, Dublin. 1875. Vol. 17, No. 373, July 1. pp. 253, 259.

Educational Buildings

Judge, P.M. (Ed)   O'Connell Schools. 150 years. 1828-1978. O'Connell Schools Union, Dublin, 1978.

Alexandra School. W.H. Parry, architect. Irish Builder, Dublin. 1886. No. 684. June 15. pp. 161-162.

Nos. 85 and 86 St. Stephen's Green. The President and Governing Body of University College, Dublin.

All Hallows College, Drumcondra. J.J. McCarthy, architect. Dublin Builder, Dublin. 1860. Vol. 2, No. 14, February 1. p. 201.

All Hallows College, Drumcondra. New chapel. G.C. Ashlin, architect. Irish Builder, Dublin. 1895. Vol. 37, No. 854, July 15. p. 31.

Diocesan seminary of the Holy Cross, Clonliffe. J. Bourke, architect. Dublin Builder. 1860. Vol. 2, No. 20, August 1. p. 31.

Illustrations to the history of the National Library of Ireland, 1877-1977. 1979. Stationery Office Dublin.

Royal College of Physicians. W.G. Murray, architect. Irish Builder, Dublin. 1862. Vol. 4, No. 59, June 1. pp. 134-135.

Royal University Buildings, Earlsfort Terrace. Irish Builder, Dublin. 1881. Vol. 23, No. 513, May 1. pp. 132, 135.

St. Andrew's Parochial School. W.K. Parry, architect. Irish Builder, Dublin. 1892. Vol. 34, No. 792, December 15. 1892. pp. 262-3.

University College Dublin and its buildings plans. Published for UCD by Browne and Nolan Ltd., Dublin, 1959.

University of Dublin, Trinity College. A short illustrated history of Trinity College and its buildings. TCD, Dublin.

THE NATIONAL LIBRARY, KILDARE STREET.

The library of the Royal Dublin Society was transferred to the state in 1877. A competition was held for the design of a suitable building to house the collection and this was won by the Deanes.

Thomas Manly Deane was the architect mainly responsible for the monumental design. His father, Thomas Newenham Deane was knighted on the opening day in 1890.

There is a photograph of the National Museum on page 42.

The drawing reproduced on the cover of this book illustrates Sir Thomas Manly Deane's design for the National Library and the National Museum. The original drawing was made by T. Raffles Brown. In the competition for the design of St. Andrew's Church, St. Andrew's Street, Raffles Brown was placed third and he subsequently completed the work commenced by Lanyon and Lynn.

The public library of St. Sepulchre, which later became known as Marsh's Library, was founded by Archibhsop Narcissus Marsh. William Robinson was responsible for the design of the original building erected to house Marsh's Library in 1702. The building was restored in 1863-69 by Sir Thomas Drew, when it was clad in stone and brick. Internally, the old carved oak book cases and decorative grilles featuring gilded mitres, still remain.

MARSH'S
LIBRARY,
ST. PATRICK'S
CLOSE.

Bibliography

Hospitals

City of Dublin Hospital, Upper Baggot Street. A.E. Murray, architect. Irish Builder, Dublin. 1892. Vol. 34, No. 792, December 15. pp. 262-3.

Jervis Street Hospital. C. Geoghegan, architect. Irish Builder, Dublin. Vol. 34, No. 650, January 15.

The Children's Hospital, Temple Street, 1872-1972. 1973. Printed by Cahill, Dublin.

Hotels

Bowen, E.   The Shelbourne. Harrap, London. 1951.

Dublin hotel architecture. Dublin Builder. 1862. Vol. 4, No. 6, November 1. p. 275.

Ship Hotel, Lower Abbey Street. W.H. Byrne, architect. Irish Builder, Dublin. 1835. Vol. 27, No. 603, February 1. p. 38.

Houses

de Breffney, B.   The houses of Ireland. Thames and Hudson, London. 1975. pp. 211-231.

Harrison, W.   Memorable Dublin houses. Illustrated guide. W. Lechie & Co. Dublin 1980. Reprinted in 1971 with a new introduction by Maurice Craig. S.R. Publishers, Wakefield, England.

Shannon, E.   The American Ambassador's residence, Dublin. Irish Heritage Series: 28. Eason & Son, Dublin. 1979.

Sheaf, N.   Iveagh House. Department of Foreign Affairs, Dublin. 1978.

Guinness Trust dwellings. R.M. Stirling, architect. 1894. Vol. 36, No. 827, June 1. p. 131.

New houses, Grafton Street, Dublin. W.M. Mitchell, architect. Irish Builder, Dublin. 1881. Vol. 23, No. 517, July 1. pp. 197, 204.

Railway Stations

Kingsbridge Station. Gifford and Craven, Ballycotton, Co. Cork. 1973.

Kingsbridge Terminus, Great Southern and Western Railway. S. Wood, architect. Dublin Builder. 1864. Vol. 6, No. 106, May 15.

Shepherd, W.E.   The Dublin South Eastern Railway. David and Charles, Newton Abbott. 1974.

OFFICE OF PUBLIC WORKS, 51, ST. STEPHEN'S GREEN.

No. 51, St. Stephen's Green, which originally housed the Museum of Irish Industry, was purchased by the Government in 1848. The Office of Public Works moved into the building in 1913.

The Loreto College was founded in 1883 and the oldest part of the convent and school buildings, facing St. Stephen's Green, survived the tragic fire which destroyed the buildings at the rear in 1986.

Catherine McAuley bought the site in Lower Baggot Street in 1827 and built a school for poor children and a hostel for working women. St. Catherine's Convent became the mother house of the Sisters of Mercy. Nuns from the convent opened a school in Goldenbridge in 1855.

Carysfort Teacher Training College, founded by the Sisters of Charity in Baggot Street in 1877, was transferred to Blackrock in 1884 where extensive buildings were erected.

ST. CATHERINE'S
CONVENT OF THE
SISTERS OF MERCY,
LOWER BAGGOT STREET.

New Buildings, Northern Railway Terminus, Amiens Street. J. Lanyon, architect. Irish Builder, Dublin. 1879. Vol. 21, No. 460, February 15. p. 52.

Bridges

Tinsley, M.E.   The bridges over the Liffey. Tinsley, Dublin. 1978.

PERIODICALS

Architectural Review. Cuairt an AR ar Bhaile Átha Cliath. The Architectural Review London. 1974.

An Taisce Journal. 1977-

Country Life. The building of Trinity College Dublin. Edward McParland. Articles reprinted from the magazine.

Dublin Historical Record. 1939-   . Dublin Builder 1859-66. Continued from 1867 onwards as the Irish Builder. 1867-1908. Title changes to the Irish Builder and Engineer (1903).

Brioscú, A.   Gypsum Journal, 46. The changing face of Dublin. The Gypsum Plasterboard Development Association, London, 1967.

Irish Georgian Society Quarterly Bulletin.

BACKGROUND REFERENCES

Beckett, J.C.   The making of the modern Ireland 1603-1923. Faber, London. 1969.

Cullen, L.M.   Six generations (Life and work in Ireland from 1790). Mercier Press, Cork. 1970.

Cullen, L.M.   Life in Ireland. Batsford, London. 1979.

Lee, J.   The modernization of Irish Society (1848-1918).

Ó Tuathaigh, G.   Ireland before the Famine (1798-1848). Gill and MacMillan, Dublin. 1972.

ST. BRIGID'S CHURCH, BLANCHARDSTOWN.

With the growth of population in County Dublin many of the existing buildings were not big enough to meet new requirements. A large number of the Eighteenth and early Nineteenth Century churches have been replaced by new ones but in other cases the original buildings have been extended to accommodate larger congregations. St. Brigid's Church, Blanchardstown, has been extended and the old church, with its graceful spire, has been preserved as part of the local scene.

Small schools, like this one in Clondalkin, are difficult to extend and/or adapt to cater for larger numbers of pupils and new educational requirements. In some cases, however, small-scale buildings of this type have been successfully adapted to other uses.

PRIMARY SCHOOL,
CLONDALKIN.

Bibliography

RECENT PUBLICATIONS

Coughlan, J.	Memories. A pictorial celebration for Dublin's Millennium. Smurfit Publications, Dublin. 1987.
Liddy, P.	Dublin be proud. Chadworth Ltd. Dublin. 1987.
Liddy, P.	Dublin today. The Irish Times. Dublin. 1984.
M'Cready, C. T.	Dublin street names. Dated and explained. Carraig Books. Blackrock, Co. Dublin. First edition 1892. Reprinted 1987.
O'Donnell, E. E.	The Annals of Dublin. Fair City. Photographs from the Francis Brown, S.J., Collection. Wolfhound Press, Dublin. 1987.
O'Donovan, J.	Life by the Liffey. A kaleidoscope of Dubliners. Gill and Macmillan. Dublin. 1986.

While some of the old public houses have been altered and enlarged beyond recognition, others still retain much of their original architectural character. Brian McEvoy, the present owner of the thatched public house in Newcastle, Co. Dublin, continues a long family tradition in the business. The general appearance of the premises has been preserved without undue alteration down through the generations.

THE THATCH
PUBLIC HOUSE,
NEWCASTLE.

DUBLIN
CIVIC
MUSEUM
SOUTH
WILLIAM
STREET.

The Dublin Civic Museum has since 1953 been located in the former City Assembly House built in 1765-71. The Dublin Corporation met here in South William Street until it moved to the former Royal Exchange building in Cork Hill, designed by Thomas Cooley and built in 1769-89. The impressive building, with its main front facing down Parliament Street, then became the City Hall. Since then some internal alterations have been made. The front balustrade and entrance steps were not part of the original design.

THE CITY HALL, FORMERLY THE ROYAL EXCHANGE, CORK HILL.

INDEX OF PERSONS
mentioned in main body of text

MANSION HOUSE, DAWSON STREET.

Joshua Dawson's house was purchased by the Corporation in 1715.

The Round Room, designed by John Semple, was added in 1821. The adjoining Supper Room was built at the same time. Dáil Éireann met in the Round Room in 1918.

Northland House, Dawson Street, built about 1770, has a brick facade with stone features and inside there is some fine decorative plasterwork. The Royal Irish Academy, founded in 1785, moved into the house in 1852. The building was extended at the rear to provide additional accommodation for libraries and meeting rooms.

ROYAL IRISH ACADEMY, 19, DAWSON STREET.

INDEX OF PERSONS
mentioned in main body of text

EARLY TWENTIETH CENTURY HOUSES, LONDON-BRIDGE ROAD.

CENTRAL
FIRE STATION.

The Central Fire Station at the corner of Pearse Street and Tara Street, has a brick and stone tower which rises to a height of almost 40 m. The building, designed specially for the Fire Service by the City Architect, was built in 1907.

Another red brick building, Tara Street Baths, has been replaced by a Swimming Pool in Townsend Street.

The Dublin Corporation Fruit and Vegetable Market, bounded by St. Mary's Lane, St. Michan Street, Chancery Street and East Arran Street, was built in 1892. The external walls are of brick and stone. They are quite elaborate in design and include some very attractive features, including decorative entrance gateways.

FRUIT AND VEGETABLE
MARKET,
ST. MICHAN STREET AND
ST. MARY'S LANE.

INDEX TO BUILDINGS
mentioned in the text
For Index to Buildings Illustrated see page 245

POWERSCOURT TOWN HOUSE, SOUTH WILLIAM STREET.

Powerscourt House, South William Street, designed by Robert Mack, was built by Lord Powerscourt in 1771-74 as his own town house. It was bought by the Commissioners of Stamp Duties in 1807 and later extended on three sides of a courtyard. In 1835 it was purchased by Ferrier Pollock who occupied the premises until they sold it for conversion into a modern shopping complex, the change affected in 1981. The original house has some fine decorative plasterwork by James McCullough.

The former Moravian Church in Lower Kevin Street is now the Sports Injury Centre. The facade, which has some interesting features, is well preserved.

The redbrick Public Library is on the opposite side of the street.

Kevin Street Garda Station is located in the medieval Archbishop's Palace of St. Sepulchre.

MORAVIAN CHURCH,
41 LOWER KEVIN STREET,
NOW THE SPORTS
INJURY CENTRE.

DOLPHIN HOUSE (FORMER DOLPHIN HOTEL), EAST ESSEX STREET.

For many years the Dolphin Hotel, with decorative brick and stone exterior, was well known to visitors to the capital. Although the hotel went out of business, the building has been preserved by converting it to use as offices. The building, designed by J. J. O'Callaghan, was built in 1887.

Sunlight Chambers was built for Lever Brothers and the coloured terra cotta frieze depicts the story of soap. Although the soap manufacturing firm no longer occupies the building the decorative facade has been preserved in good condition and continues to be a source of interest to the passers-by.

SUNLIGHT CHAMBERS, 21, PARLIAMENT STREET.

SICK AND INDIGENT ROOMKEEPERS' SOCIETY, 2, PALACE STREET.

The Sick and Indigent Roomkeepers' Society, founded in 1790, moved to 2, Palace Street in 1851. Down through the years this voluntary body has rendered great assistance to many of Dublin's poor. The organisation's premises is now the last remaining house in the short street which leads from Dame Street to Dublin Castle.

A branch of Allied Irish Banks is located on the opposite side of the street.

IRISH AGRICULTURAL WHOLESALE SOCIETY LIMITED, 151 THOMAS STREET.

INDEX TO BUILDINGS (Contd.)

**A complete Index to Buildings Illustrated
begins on page 245**

IVEAGH
HOUSE,
ST. STEPHEN'S
GREEN.

The original building designed for Bishop Clayton by Richard Cassels was purchased by John Philpot Curran in 1809. The property changed hands several times and in 1856 it was purchased by Benjamin Lee Guinness who had extensive additions (incorporating adjoining houses) and alterations carried out. A new Portland stone facade was built in 1866 to the design of J. F. Fuller. In 1896 a ballroom, designed by William Young, was added to the amenities of Iveagh House. The building is now the headquarters of the Department of Foreign Affairs.

The granite-faced 86, St. Stephen's Green was built for Richard Chapel Whaley in 1765. The decorataive plasterwork was carried out by Robert West. In 1854 the house was acquired by Dr. Henry Newman for the Catholic University. No. 85, also acquired for University purposes, was originally known as Clanwilliam House. It has fine decorative palsterwork by the Francini Brothers. Both houses were restored in 1918 and again in the 1940s. The Aula Maxima was built beside Clanwilliam House in 1878 through the munificence of Paul Cardinal Cullen. The three properties are known collectively as Newman House. University Church, beside 86, St. Stephen's Green, was designed by John Hungerford Pollen and built in 1855-56.

NEWMAN
HOUSE,
ST. STEPHEN'S
GREEN.

PHOTOGRAPHIC SURVEY
(continued)

The Photographic Survey in the second part of the book is a continuation of the illustrations in the first part. The above list is a brief guide to the types of buildings illustrated in the second part. A comprehensive alphabetical index to all the buildings illustrated in both parts of the book begins on page 245.

GRAND
CANAL
BETWEEN
BAGGOT
STREET
AND
LEESON
STREET.

Work on the Grand Canal, under the direction of Thomas Omer, engineer of the Board of Inland Navigation, who encountered many difficulties both technical and financial, was commenced in 1756 and finished about 1804.

The new waterway was a great boom in the early part of the Nineteenth Century but after the building of the railways in the early 1840s it declined in importance.

These houses, which faced the Grand Canal, have been replaced by an office block.

TERRACE OF HOUSES, MESPIL ROAD.

IRISH PERMANENT BUILDING SOCIETY, 1, LOWER O'CONNELL STREET.

The premises on the corner of O'Connell Street and Lower Abbey Street was designed by W. H. Byrne for the Hibernian Bank. The bank later moved to new premises on the site of the Grand Central Cinema in O'Connell Street and the prominent corner building was acquired by the Irish Permanent Building Society.

The chief office of the Society is now in Edmund Farrell House, on the site of St. Vincent's Hospital, St. Stephen's Green, founded by Mother Mary Aikenhead in 1834. The hospital moved to its new premises in Elm Park in 1970.

CHIEF OFFICE,
IRISH PERMANANT
BUILDING SOCIETY,
EDMUND FARRELL HOUSE,
56, ST. STEPHEN'S GREEN.

Dublin has suffered the loss of many of its theatres. The Queen's Theatre provided a temporary home for the National Theatre Company when the new Abbey was being planned and constructed following the fire which destroyed the old theatre building. The original theatre in Brunswick Street (now Pearse Street) was called the Adelphi Theatre. It was opened in 1829.

The Capitol Theatre, like the last Theatre Royal, served as a theatre, concert hall and cinema. Both the Queen's and the Capitol as well as the Theatre Royal were demolished to make way for new commercial buildings.

McKenzie's store, next to the Queen's Theatre, was destroyed in a fire and replaced by an office block (Oisín House).

CAPITOL THEATRE,
PRINCE'S STREET.

ROYAL IRISH ACADEMY OF MUSIC, 36, 37 & 38 WESTLAND ROW. In its early years the Academy of Music was based in 18 St. Stephen's Green. In order to accommodate its growing needs it moved to Westland Row where it is at present.

From 1883 to 1910 Academy pupils' concerts were held in the Great Hall of the Royal University in Earlsfort Terrace, now the National Concert Hall.

No. 36 Westland Row, now part of the premises occupied by the Royal Irish Academy of Music, was built in 1771 by Nicholas Trench of Fassaroe, Co. Wicklow, for his own use. The Earl of Conyngham later acquired it as his town house. Following this it passed into the possession of Sir George Aylmer of Newcastle Lyons. The Academy, founded in 1856, moved into the house in 1871, having purchased it from Mr. de Burgh of St. Doulough's. A band room extension was built in 1890. This was later enlarged to become the present Dagg Hall. The RIAM acquired the adjoining houses (nos. 37 and 38) in 1911. No. 36, with its fine decorative plasterwork by Michael Stapleton, has been carefully preserved. The wrought iron balustrade is an attractive feature of the main staircase and there is an unusual Gothic fireplace in the Organ Room. There are fine grisaille medallions in the front ground floor room and other painted medallions in the manner of Angelica Kaufmann in the first floor room over the entrance hall.

Ceol-Acadamh Ríoga na hÉireann.

ROYAL IRISH ACADEMY OF MUSIC, WESTLAND ROW.

There is a continuous Nineteenth-Century facade of redbrick and terra cotta in Baggot Street, from the corner of Haddington Road to Eastmoreland Place.

The design of the facades in Upper Baggot Street is varied but the consistent use of brick and stone throughout gives the upper part of the buildings a unified appearance. The modern shop fronts at street level, however, compete with one another and draw attention from the superstructure.

In Dawson Street the upper part of the Brown Thomas building designed by A. E. Murray, has some attractive detail.

The Brown Thomas buildings in Grafton Street date back to the middle of the Nineteenth Century. Some of the old shop fronts in the extended premises have been restored.

UPPER PART
OF FACADE,
BROWN THOMAS,
DAWSON STREET.

UPPER
STOREYS,
ARNOTT'S
STORE,
GRAFTON
STREET.

*There is a well-balanced combination of brick and stone in the facade of Arnott's store in Grafton
Street.*

The original Switzer store designed by Rawson Carroll was built in 1859. The extended Art Noveau
facade, designed by Donnelly and Moore, was built in 1913.

*Eason's shop in O'Connell Street, a reinforced concrete building with stone facing, was designed by
the English architect R. H. Rutven. Clery's store, on the opposite side of the street, is a steel framed
building with stone facing.*

The facade
of glazed
terra cotta
is typical
of English
store design
of the 1920s.

UPPER
STOREYS,
FORMER
BURTON'S
STORE,
CORNER
OF SOUTH
GREAT
GEORGE'S
STREET.

LOMBARD & ULSTER BANK, 1 DAWSON STREET.

The building, now occupied by the Lombard and Ulster Bank at the corner of Dawson Street and Nassau Street, was designed by Peddie and Washington Browne of Edinburgh for the North British Assurance Company.

The former Genealogical Office (originally the Office of Arms) and Bedford Tower, Dublin Castle, are believed to have been designed by Thomas Ivory. The building was erected in 1750-60 but the top storey was added in the Nineteenth Century. The Genealogical Office is now located in the former Kildare Street Club premises in Kildare Street.

The statue of Fortune over the western gateway and the statue of Justice over the eastern gateway are by Van Nost.

George's Hall in Dublin Castle was built in 1911.

FORMER
GENEOLOGICAL OFFICE
AND BEDFORD TOWER,
DUBLIN CASTLE.

THOMAS PRIOR HOUSE, SIMMONSCOURT ROAD, BALLSBRIDGE.

The Masonic Female Orphan School building, purchased by the Royal Dublin Society in 1972 and named after one of the Society's founders, Thomas Prior, was designed by McCurdy and Mitchell, architects, and built in 1882. The property has since been sold by the RDS.

The first Spring Show by the RDS in Ballsbridge was held in 1881, the site leased from the Earl of Pembroke.

The nearby Convent of the Poor Clares was built on part of the grounds of Simmonscourt Castle.

Many of the important buildings of the Nineteenth and early Twentieth Centuries were crowned with attractive features rising above the general roof level, as in the case of Thomas Prior House. Penneys' (formerly Todd Burns') store in Mary Street has a much larger copper dome rising above the parapet.

PENNEYS' (FORMERLY TODD BURNS' STORE), MARY STREET.

The Garda Station in Pearse Street was originally designed (1912-15) for the Dublin Metropolitan Police (merged with An Garda Síochána in 1925) by Andrew Robinson in accordance with the brief drawn up by the Office of Public Works in 1838. Interesting features of the Scottish Baronial style facade of County Dublin granite are the carved heads at the entrances.

The Store Street police station was built in 1880.

The lower part of the Iveagh Market, Francis Street, built in 1907, is faced with stone and the upper part is faced with brick. The ground floor openings have semi-circular heads and there is a circular window in the middle of the tympanum.

Iveagh Markets,
Francis Street,
were designed
by Frederick
Hicks.

IVEAGH
MARKETS,
FRANCIS
STREET.

GARDA STATION, FITZGIBBON STREET.

The stone and brick facade of Fitzgibbon Street Garda Station has some interesting features. The top storey rises above the main cornice and the ground floor is faced with rusticated stonework. Pilasters above the arched main entrance are positioned in front of the two intermediate storeys.

Clontarf Garda Station was built in 1909.

Fitzgibbon House, with its decorative brick and stone facade, was built in 1863. It is a most unusual design and shows a remarkable use of brickwork to create a colourful decorative effect, although it is somewhat dwarfed by the nearby Garda Station, a large gray building on the same side of the road.

FITZGIBBON HOUSE, FITZGIBBON STREET.

127

PROVINCIAL BANK CHAMBERS
COLLEGE STREET
AND
WESTMORELAND STREET.

The building on the corner of College Street and Westmoreland Street, designed by the Deanes, was originally commissioned by Scottish Widows Insurance Company but it was later acquired for use as bank premises. The carefully detailed Romanesque building fits in well with its surroundings. It is faced with Mansfield stone imported from Nottinghamshire, England.

The building was bought by the Provincial Bank and named Provincial Bank Chambers. It is now owned by AIB.

A firm of stockbrokers occupies 2 College Street (on right in picture). Further down the street, 5 College Street is now occupied by a branch of AIB. This elaborate building is illustrated on page 161.

The tall red brick building on the corner of Grafton Street and Chatham Street is still used for its original purpose and is now a branch of the Allied Irish Bank. While the ground floor fronts of most Grafton Street premises have been greatly altered since first built this one has been retained.

ALLIED IRISH BANK,
GRAFTON STREET.

128

HOUSE, ELY PLACE

With the development of the capital houses in the inner city were gradually converted for commercial and professional use. Residential areas, like Ely Place and Hume Street, were gradually taken over for business purposes. The cul-de-sac which forms part of Ely Place, once a quiet residential area, gradually became part of the busy city scene. Ely House, built by Lord Ely in 1775, has been well preserved.

The facade of this tall business premises in St. Andrew Street is divided horizontally into four parts. The building, located beside St. Andrew's Church, was erected in 1877 and for a period was used by a firm of auctioneers.

PREMISES,
ST. ANDREW'S STREET,
BUILT IN 1877.

BUILDING ON CORNER OF FISHAMBLE STREET AND LORD EDWARD STREET.

The extensive brick building on the corner of Fishamble Streete extends down Lord Edward Street and it includes the premises of the Dublin Working Boys' Home and the Harding Technical School.

The building has been purchased by the Union of Students in Ireland for use as a students' hostel.

Near the other end of the street, on the opposite side, is the Carnegie Trust Child Welfare Centre which was completed in 1927

The former premises of Dublin Corporation Public Library Service is no longer in use and it has been partly demolished.

Public libraries were opened in Thomas Street and Capel Street in 1884.

FORMER PREMISES OF DUBLIN CORPORATION PUBLIC LIBRARY SERVICE, THOMAS STREET.

OFFICE BUILDING,
ANGLESEA STREET.

This elaborate facade with its first floor bay window, brightens up Anglesea Street, the narrow thoroughfare which connects Dame Street and Fleet Street.

The Stock Exchange building in Anglesea Street was built about 1878.

There is a strong resemblance between this facade in Merrion Row and the one in Anglesea Street illustrated above. Both premises are located in fairly narrow busy streets but nevertheless they attract considerable attention.

OFFICES,
MERRION ROW.

TREASURY BUILDINGS, DUBLIN CASTLE.

A view of Dublin Castle by James del Vecchio, published in 1816 includes the Treasury, facing the new chapel. This brick and stone terrace has been preserved. The Cross Block, separating the Upper and Lower Castle Yards, dating back to 1716, was rebuilt in 1961-64.

The Royal Barracks (now known as Collins' Barracks) was designed by Thomas Burgh, Surveyor General, and built on a commanding site north of the Liffey, in the early part of the Eighteenth Century. The site was granted by Dublin Corporation to the Duke of Ormond who transferred it to the State as a site for the barracks.

The building, now known as Clancy Barracks, was built on the south bank of the Liffey at Islandbridge in the last quarter of the Eighteenth Century. Portobello (now Cathal Brugha) Barracks was built in the early part of the Nineteenth Century, followed about twelve years later by Beggars Bush Barracks. Other barracks include Marlborough (McKee) and Wellington (Griffith) and Arbour Hill.

COLLINS'
(FORMERLY
ROYAL)
BARRACKS.

ST. STEPHEN'S GREEN.

In the Nineteenth and Twentieth Centuries important developments took place on the periphery of St. Stephen's Green and in the streets opening off it. In recent times the east side of the Green has undergone more change than the other three sides. Only the Unitarian Church, the College of Surgeons and a pair of other buildings have survived from the last two Centuries. The corner buildings shown here have been replaced by offices.

The Shelbourne Hotel now incorporates some adjoining houses, one of which has an access archway, a feature typical of many other houses throughout the city.

Another picture of the Shelbourne Hotel is reproduced on page 150 and other hotels are illustrated on pages 150-155.

SHELBOURNE HOTEL, ST. STEPHEN'S GREEN.

The Campanile, Trinity College, designed by Sir Charles Lanyon, was erected in 1852. It was built on the site of All Hallows' Priory. It is 30 m high. The heads of Homer, Socrates, Plato and Demosthenes are carved on the keystones.

Keane and Sanderson and Theodore Jacobsen were involved in the design of the imposing West Front (1752-59) of Trinity College which faces College Green. The East facade of the main block, built of Wicklow granite and Portland stone, and the entrance archway from College Green through Regent House in the centre of the block can be seen from the Front Square, also known as Parliament Square.

FRONT
SQUARE,
TRINITY
COLLEGE.

VIEW THROUGH THE CAMPANILE, TRINITY COLLEGE.

The view through the Campanile, Trinity College, shows the rear of the central feature, Regent House, which accommodated the College Museum during the Nineteenth Century.

The view from the Campanile, looking in the opposite direction, shows the Rubrics, separating Library Square and New Square, built at the beginning of the Eighteenth Century. The top storey, rebuilt in 1891, features Dutch gables. The facade is faced with red brick but the rear is finished with stucco.

THE RUBRICS, TRINITY COLLEGE.

The chapel on the north side of the Front Square in Trinity College, was designed by Sir William Chambers and Graham Myers and completed in 1793. Between the Corinthian portico and the nave there is a large vestibule. The chapel has some excellent stucco decoration by Michael Stapleton and Nineteenth Century stained glass. There is a graceful curved balcony and decorative wall panelling.

The adjacent Dining Hall (1734), designed by Richard Cassels, has an interesting collection of paintings dating from 1800. The building was extended on the west side in 1891. It was reconstructed after a disastrous fire in 1984.

The Examination Hall (completed about 1790) on the south side of the Front Square was designed by Sir William Chambers. Decorative plasterwork was executed by Michael Stapleton. The building is also used as a concert hall. An organ made by W. Telford was installed in 1839.

DINING HALL, TRINITY COLLEGE.

PRINTING HOUSE, TRINITY COLLEGE.

The Printing House, Trinity College, was designed by Richard Cassels and built in 1734. It was the gift of the Church of Ireland Bishop of Clogher. Designed in the form of a Greek Doric temple it provided accommodation for the University Press but is now used for other purposes.

The design of the building was the first commission given to the architect in Dublin. He later designed Tyrone House and Leinster House.

An example of the work of Sir Thomas Drew, architect, may be seen in Trinity College.

The Graduates' Memorial Building separating Library Square from Botany Bay in Trinity College was built in celebration of the tercentenary of the University. It provides accommodation for activities of various college societies, including meetings, lectures and debates.

The building was paid for by subscriptions from graduates of the college.

GRADUATES' MEMORIAL BUILDING, TRINITY COLLEGE.

The Provost's House facing onto Grafton Street was built in 1759-60 with sandstone imported from Liverpool. It was designed by the Earl of Cork and Burlington, Richard Boyle, with additions by John Smyth. It has very fine reception rooms, including an elaborately decorated salon about 15 m long. An interesting feature is the octagonal staircase. Some minor alterations and additions were carried out in the Nineteenth Century.

The Old Library, Trinity College, designed by Sir Thomas Burgh, Chief Engineer and Surveyor General of Fortifications, was opened in 1732. In the early Nineteenth Century the two upper storeys were faced with granite. In the middle of that Century a barrel vault was erected over the Long Room on the top floor and at the end of the century the open arcade at ground level was closed to provide additional storage space.

THE OLD LIBRARY, TRINITY COLLEGE.

SCHOOL OF PHYSICS, TRINITY COLLEGE.

The School of Physics is located at the east end of College Park. Also located on this part of the campus are the Departments of Chemistry, Anatomy, Zoology, Physiology, Surgery and Pharmacology. The buildings, which incorporate lecture halls and laboratories, were erected in the last quarter of the Nineteenth Century.

The building which is now occupied by the Academy Cinema and some shops was the headquarters of the Antient Concerts' Society in the middle of the Nineteenth Century.

ANTIENT CONCERT ROOMS, NOW ACADEMY CINEMA, PEARSE STREET.

MATER MISERICORDIAE HOSPITAL, ECCLES STREET.

The Mater Misericordiae Hospital, Eccles Street, founded by the Sisters of Mercy, was built in 1861. The central block with its Classical portico and the large chapel within the hospital complex was designed by John Bourke. The East Wing was built in 1871.

St. Mary's Hospital, Phoenix Park, was originally the Royal Hibernian Military School. The main building was erected in 1766 but this was enlarged in 1803-13 in accordance with plans drawn up by Francis Johnston, architect. The chapel, designed by Thomas Cooley, was built in 1771.

In 1948 St. Mary's was opened as a chest hospital but since 1962 it cares for geriatric patients.

ST. MARY'S HOSPITAL, PHOENIX PARK.

FORMER MATER PRIVATE NURSING HOME, ECCLES STREET.

The former Mater Private Nursing Home occupied a terrace of houses in Eccles Street and the facade rendered in sand and cement, presenting unified appearance. The new Mater Private Hospital in Eccles Street was opened in 1985 but the old building is still in use for medical services.

The foundation stone of Sir Patrick Dun's Hospital was laid out on the site in Artichoke Road, now Grand Canal Street, in 1803 and the building was completed in 1808. The design of the granite-faced building was influenced by George Papworth.

The hospital building is now owned by the Institute of Clinical Pharmacology and used for its purposes.

FORMER
SIR
PATRICK
DUN'S
HOSPITAL,
GRAND
CANAL
STREET.

ROYAL COLLEGE
OF SURGEONS,
ST. STEPHEN'S
GREEN.

The Royal College of Surgeons, St. Stephen's Green, designed by Edward Parke, was built about 1806. It was extended in 1827 in accordance with plans drawn up by William Murray. Recently extensive additions have been built in York Street but the original building, with its granite and Portland stone facade to St. Stephen's Green, is an important part of the College complex. The statues of Apollo, Hygeia and Escalpius which stand above the pediment, are by Edward Smyth.

The South Dublin Lying-in Hospital was founded in 1883. The original hospital buildings in Holles Street were replaced by the National Maternity Hospital completed in 1937 to the design of W. H. Byrne and Sons, architects.

The Gasometer on Sir John Rogerson's Quay, takes from the appearance of the building as viewed from Fitzwilliam Street.

NATIONAL
MATERNITY
HOSPITAL,
HOLLES
STREET.

ROYAL CITY OF DUBLIN HOSPITAL, BAGGOT STREET.

The facade of the Royal City of Dublin Hospital, Baggot Street, was designed by Albert E. Murray. Set back from the line of adjacent buildings, dating from the Nineteenth Century, it is constructed of brick and terra cotta. The hospital building was completed in 1898 and replaced an earlier one opened in 1832, which consisted of converted houses.

The Nurses' Home belonging to the Baggot Street Hospital, faces towards St. Mary's Road. It was also designed by A. E. Murray and the external appearance of the building is in similar style to that of the hospital and is constructed of the same materials.

The Royal City of Dublin Hospital no longer functions as an acute general hospital. A community health centre is now located in part of the building.

Many other hospitals have been altered and extended since they were built. These include St. Kevin's (renamed St. James's) Hospital (1922), formerly the South Dublin Union; Dr. Steeven's Hospital (1721-33) designed by Thomas Burgh; the Rotunda Lying-in Hospital (1751); and the Meath Hospital (1753).

St. Laurence's (formerly the Richmond) Hospital includes some buildings designed by Francis Johnston as well as red brick buildings designed by Bachelor and Hicks, architects.

NURSES' HOME,
BAGGOT STREET
HOSPITAL.

DR. STEEVEN'S
HOSPITAL.

Dr. Steeven's Hospital, designed by Thomas Burgh, was founded in 1720 and the building in Steeven's Lane was opened in 1733. A number of additions were made in later years, including the erection of the clock tower and the building of the red brick Nurses' Home. The hospital is now closed.   The buildings are to be put to new use.

The nearby St. Patrick's Hospital (also known as Swift's, as it was founded by Dean Swift) was opened in 1757.Designed by George Semple, it was extended in 1778 by George Semple, subsequently by other architects.

NURSES' HOME,
DR. STEEVEN'S
HOSPITAL.

144

JERVIS STREET
HOSPITAL.

Some of the
Nineteenth
Century
buildings
of Jervis St.
Hospital
were
designed
by Charles
Geoghegan.

The hospital in Jervis Street has been closed down and the buildings, comprising general hospital, nursing home, convent, doctor's residence and school of nursing which stand on a site of approximately one hectare are to be put to new use.

The Richmond, Hardwicke and Whitworth Hospitals in North Brunswick Street were founded in the beginning of the Nineteenth Century. The early buildings were designed by Francis Johnston. Development was continued in the Nineteenth and early Twentieth Centuries. Elaborate brick-faced buildings with verandahs and copper domes were designed by Bachelor and Hicks, architects.

RICHMOND,
WHITWORTH,
HARDWICKE,
NOW ST.
LAURENCE'S
HOSPITAL,
NORTH
BRUNSWICK
STREET.

CITY OF DUBLIN, SKIN AND CANCER HOSPITAL, HUME STREET.

Set in between the brick-fronted houses in Hume Street is the painted facade of the City of Dublin Skin and Cancer Hospital which was founded in 1911. It now func-tions mainly as a day care centre.

In the Nineteenth Century a number of clubs moved into premises on the north side of St. Stephen's Green. The Hibernian United Services Club moved from Foster Place into the house built for the Bishop of Kilalla, Samuel Hutchinson, in 1847. Inter-nal alterations were carried out and in the 1880s the building was faced with Dolphin's Barn brick and bay windows added.

In the present University and Kildare Street Club premises, 17 St. Stephen's Green, there is decorative plasterwork by Michael Stapleton. Milltown House, as it is called, was built by John Leeson and acquired by the University Club in 1850. The premises of the Bankers' Club, 92/93 St. Stephen's Green, was built in 1820.

The front of the United Services Club (No. 8) dates from 1754 and that of the St. Stephen's Green Club from 1756.

CLUBS, SAINT STEPHEN'S GREEN.

ROYAL
HOSPITAL,
KILMAINHAM.

Kilmainham Jail, designed by Sir John Traille, was built in 1796. In the middle of the Nineteenth Century alterations were carried out to the design of Major Jebb who was also the architect of Mountjoy Jail.

The design of the adjacent Courthouse has been attributed to George Papworth.

The Royal Hospital for veteran soldiers, designed by Sir William Robinson, was built in 1680. Planned around a rectangle there are open colonnades on three sides of the courtyard. It has an elegant clock tower and sundial. Special features of the interior are the decorative ceiling in the dining hall and the wood carving and ironwork in the chapel. The ceiling of the chapel was replaced in 1901 under the direction of Sir Thomas Drew, architect. The Royal Hospital was restored and opened in 1985 as a cultural centre.

The Nineteenth Century entrance gateway, designed by Francis Johnston and erected at Barrack Bridge in 1812, was moved from that site to Kilmainham in 1846.

ENTRANCE GATEWAY,
ROYAL HOSPITAL,
KILMAINHAM.

The Royal College of Physicians was granted its Royal Charter in 1890. The College building, designed by William G. Murray, was built about 1862. The original stonework did not weather well and it was necessary to carry out a major refacing in the 1960s.

ROYAL COLLEGE OF PHYSICIANS, 6, KILDARE STREET.

OFFICE BUILDING ON CORNER OF UPPER FOWNES STREET AND DAME STREET.

The elaborate office building on the corner of Upper Fownes Street and Dame Street, designed by Deane and Woodward, has some fine decorative features. An interesting feature is the stepped window to the staircase on the Fownes Street elevation.

Amiens Street Station, now Connolly Station, was designed by William Deane Butler, architect, and built for the Dublin and Drogheda Railway in 1844.

Other railway stations are illustrated on page 192.

CONNOLLY STATION, AMIENS STREET.

GRESHAM
HOTEL, UPPER
O'CONNELL
STREET.

The Gresham Hotel dates back to 1817. Various alterations and additions were carried out from time to time and in 1906 the Aberdeen Hall was built. The building was destroyed in 1922 but rebuilt under the direction of the London architect, Robert Atkinson, and reopened in 1927.

The Shelbourne Hotel was built in 1820 on the site of Kerry House, residence of Lord Shelbourne. The hotel was altered and extended and an ornate facade built in 1866 to the design of John S. McCurdy.

SHELBOURNE HOTEL,
ST. STEPHEN'S
GREEN.

The Royal Hibernian Hotel, Dawson Street, opened in 1751, was used as a staging post for Bianconi's coach service. The building was altered and extended many times throughout the Nineteenth Century. Finally, it was closed in 1982, demolished and replaced by the new Hibernian Way development.

A number of other Dublin hotels, including the old Jury's Hotel in Dame Street and the Salthill Hotel in Monkstown, have been demolished to make way for new buildings. The Royal Marine Hotel, Dún Laoghaire, designed by J. S. McCurdy, has been altered and extended but the facade of the original building has been retained. The Spa Hotel, Lucan, which opened in 1891, has been altered and much enlarged.

In addition to the Royal Hibernian Hotel there were other hotels in Dawson Street in the Nineteenth Century. Macken's Royal Mail Coach Hotel was one of them. Another was Morrison's, at the bottom of the street facing Trinity College.

DEMOLITION
OF THE ROYAL
HIBERNIAN HOTEL.

151

PORTOBELLO HOUSE

Portobello House was built in 1807 as an hotel to serve passengers using the Grand Canal. Subsequently it was used for a period as a nursing home and since its restoration it is used as office accommodation.

PORTOBELLO HOUSE
BEFORE RESTORATION.

The red brick University Hall in Hatch Street, designed by William Powell, was built in 1913. The hostel has an internal courtyard and there is a small chapel with stained glass by Evie Hone.

UNIVERSITY
HALL,
HATCH
STREET.

MAGEOUGH
HOME,
COWPER
ROAD,
RATHGAR.

The Mageough Home, Cowper Road, Rathgar, was founded in 1878 under the will of Elizabeth Mageough "for the habitation, support and clothing of aged females professing the Protestant Faith". It is an extensive complex of red brick buildings, including many dwelling units, a chapel and various facilities, all part of unified design.

The nearby Temple Road and other roads in the vicinity were developed in the middle of the Nineteenth Century.

The Hall at No. 4 Northumberland Road, built in 1899, was owned by the Orange Order until it was sold to the Irish Cancer Society in 1983. St. Stephen's School, on the opposite side of the road, was associated with St. Stephen's Church of Ireland, Mount Street Crescent, but it is now a Training Centre run by the City of Dublin Vocational Education Committee.

Northumberland Road was first opened up in 1832 when there were already houses in Pembroke Road and Upper Baggot Street. The first horse-drawn trams ran from Northumberland Road to Blackrock in 1870. Electric trams were put on this route about twenty years later.

FORMER
CHURCH
HALL,
NOW
IRISH
CANCER
SOCIETY
OFFICES,
NEAR
MOUNT
STREET
BRIDGE.

GATE
LODGE,
CLONTARF
CASTLE.

Clontarf Castle was founded by the Knights Templars in the Twelfth Century. The building was reconstructed for T. C. F. Vernon in 1837 under the direction of William Vitruvius Morrison. It is now an entertainment centre.

CLONTARF
CASTLE.

THE FIVE LAMPS, NORTH STRAND.

The Five Lamps were erected at the North Strand in 1797 as a monument to General Henry Hall who served in the Indian Army. It is located near Alborough House, Portland Row, belonging to Telecom Éireann. This impressive building was originally a dwelling house but it later provided accommodation for a boarding school named the Feinaglian Institute.

Alborough House, designed by Sir William Chambers, was built at the end of the Eighteenth Century.

The lamp standards on the parapet of Grattan Bridge each feature a pair of dolphins. As in the case of the Five Lamps the original lamp shades have been replaced. The bridge was built in 1874.

LAMP STANDARD
ON THE PARAPET
OF GRATTAN
BRIDGE.

STATUE, KILDARE PLACE,
KILDARE STREET.

The statue of William Conyngham, Fourth Baron Plunket, Archbishop of Dublin, stands in Kildare Place, near the National Museum.

The four lamp-holding statues standing on the area balustrade of the Shelbourne Hotel, facing St. Stephen's Green, are admired by visitors from all parts of the world. Cast in France, the figures are Egyptian in character.

STATUE,
SHELBOURNE HOTEL,
ST. STEPHEN'S GREEN.

PARNELL MONUMENT, UPPER O'CONNELL STREET.

The foundation stone of the monument to Charles Stewart Parnell at the north end of Upper O'Connell Street was laid in 1899. The triangular obelisk is in pink Galway stone and the statue is the work of Augustus St. Gaudens.

On the corner facing O'Connell Street is the Rotunda, converted to use as a cinema in 1910 and still in use for that purpose. The Irish Volunteers were founded at a meeting held in the Rotunda in 1913.

The Rotunda (now the Ambassador Cinema) was designed by John Ensor and built about 1757. External improvements were carried out by James Gandon in 1786. Adjoining the Rotunda is the Gate Theatre (formerly the New Assembly Rooms), Cavendish Row, designed by Richard Johnston and built in 1786. Internal alterations were carried out in the Twentieth Century to adapt tne building for use as a theatre. Parnell, formerly Rutland Square, was laid out in 1757.

157

STATUE OF SIR BENJAMIN LEE GUINNESS OUTSIDE ST. PATRICK'S CATHEDRAL.

Sir Benjamin Lee Guinness financed the restoration of St. Patrick's Cathedral completed in 1864. This is duly acknowledged by the testimonial erected outside the building.

The brewer was also associated with restoration work carried out in the nearby Marsh's Library.

Sir Henry Roe, distiller, financed the restoration of Christ Church.

The statue of Sir Benjamin Lee Guinness is by John Henry Foley.

The Coburg Gardens, bounded by Earlsfort Terrace, Hatch Street and Harcourt Street were opened to the public in 1817. Benjamin Guinness, one-time owner of Iveagh House, bought the gardens and leased them to the Dublin Exhibition Palace and Winter Gardens. They were remodelled by the architect Ninian Nevin and later bought back by the Guinness family.

Iveagh Gardens, which were part of the original Coburg Gardens, passed into the care of University College Dublin and will eventually form part of the National Concert Hall complex.

A number of Nineteenth Century features survive in the Iveagh Gardens. The Coburg Gardens were part of the grounds of Clonmel House, Harcourt Street, and were the site of Exhibitions of 1865 and 1872.

STATUE, IVEAGH GARDENS.

STATUE OF LECKY,
HISTORIAN,
TRINITY COLLEGE.

The statue of William Edward Hartpole Lecky, between the Campanile and the Graduates' Memorial Building and facing the front square, was executed by W. Gascombe John, ARA, in 1906. The historian was born in Dublin in 1838.

The statue of George Salmon, Regius Professor of Divinity, Provost of Trinity College, 1888-1904, faces the Front Square of the University, which is entered through the stone archway under Regent House.

STATUE OF
GEORGE SALMON,
PROVOST OF T.C.D.,
1888-1904.

BANK OF IRELAND

The walls are of Ballynockan granite with decorative features in Portland stone.

The Parliament House, College Green, was bought by the Bank of Ireland after the passing of the Act of Union in 1801. The building was adapted by Francis Johnston who also designed the annexe in Foster Place. The foundation of the building had been laid in 1729; the eastern front, designed by James Gandon, was built in 1785; the western front by Robert Parke, was built in 1787. Parke also designed an extension to the west side in Foster Place in 1794.

Between the Ionic columns of the Bank of Ireland and the end pavilion of the west front of Trinity College, can be seen a row of buildings in College Street. No. 5, in the centre, is the former Provincial (now Allied Irish) Bank, designed by William George Murray, and built in 1868.*

*Illustrated and described on opposite page.

COLLEGE STREET,
SEEN BETWEEN
BANK OF IRELAND
AND
TRINITY COLLEGE.

160

ALLIED IRISH (FORMERLY PROVINCIAL) BANK, 5, COLLEGE STREET.

The Provincial (now Allied Irish) Bank, 5, College Street, designed by William George Murray, was built in 1868. It is a simple classical building with a deep relief tympanum by Samuel Lynn above the two-storey high Corinthian columns. Inside the building there is a lofty Banking Hall with decorative plasterwork.

The carving depicts the Guardian of Banking in the centre supported on the left by the Spirit of Commerce and Manufacture and on the right by that of Agriculture.

DETAIL OF THE DEEP RELIEF TYMPANUM BY SAMUEL LYNN.

AIB (FORMERLY PROVINCIAL BANK), 5, COLLEGE STREET.

The Northern Bank bought the Hibernian Bank premises at the corner of Church Lane and College Green in 1879. The original building was designed in the Italian Renaissance style by William George Murray. Later additions and alterations were carried out under the direction of Sir Thomas Drew, William H. Byrne and other architects. On the right is the former Royal Bank (now AIB), built in 1893.

NORTHERN BANK
(Formerly Hibernian Bank)

ALLIED IRISH BANK
(Formerly Royal Bank)
Charles Geoghegan, architect

DAME
STREET

COLLEGE
GREEN

BANK OF IRELAND
(Formerly National Bank)

ULSTER BANK

COMMERCIAL BUILDINGS.

To meet the growing need for accommodation for brokers, etc. the Commercial Buildings, designed by Edward Park, were erected in Dame Street at the end of the Eighteenth Century. A stone building in the Classical manner, it had an attractive courtyard. Although the granite stones of the old building were numbered with a view to their use in the rebuilding of the structure as part of the Central Bank development this idea was abandoned and a replica building was erected to face the bank plaza and not towards Dame Street as the original building did.

OFFICES,
DAME
STREET.

FORMER NEWCOMEN'S
BANK, NOW MUNICIPAL
BUILDINGS,
CORK HILL,
CASTLE STREET.

Newcomen's Bank, now Municipal
Buildings, Castle Street, was designed
by Thomas Ivory and built in 1781. The
facade was duplicated and the central
porch built in 1856-58. The second half
of the building is a perfect match for the
first and the addition of the porch
resolves the aesthetic problem of
duality.

Guinness and Mahon Ltd. is one of the oldest merchant banks
in Ireland. It was founded in 1836 by Robert Guinness and
John Ross Mahon. It first opened in South Frederick Street
and moved to College Green in 1854. The firm moved to yet
another four-storey building, 17 College Green, in 1881. Eight
years later Guinness Mahon expanded into No. 16 and in 1931
the two buildings were replaced by a single five-storey building
incorporating two of the rooms from the original premises.

GUINNESS & MAHON LIMITED,
17, COLLEGE GREEN, DUBLIN.

DALY'S CLUBHOUSE, (NOW OFFICES), 3-4 COLLEGE GREEN.

Daly's Clubhouse, located between Foster Place and Anglesea Street, was designed by Francis Johnston and built in 1790. Daly's was described as the smartest club in Dublin, where blinds were drawn at midday and gambling started by candlelight. Duels fought in Phoenix Park were also arranged in the premises. The wings have been replaced and alterations have been made to the upper part of the central block but the original granite facade with its untapered Ionic columns has been preserved even though the interior has been altered to meet modern requirements.

The photographs below show alterations in progress, at different times, on the buildings between Foster Place and Anglesea Street. In the centre can be seen the original facade of Daly's Club. On the extreme left is Jury's Hotel on the corner of Anglesea Street and Dame Street, which has since been replaced by an office block. In the picture on the right is the bronze statue of Henry Grattan by John Henry Foley who was also the sculptor of the statues of Oliver Goldsmith (1864) and Edmund Burke (1868) which stand in front of Trinity College.

The statue of Henry Grattan, by John Henry Foley, was erected in College Green in 1876.

The statues of Edmund Burke and Oliver Goldsmith, in front of Trinity College, and the statue of Daniel O'Connell in O'Connell Street, are also by the same sculptor.

| JURY'S HOTEL (since replaced) | 3/4 COLLEGE GREEN (DALY'S CLUB) | STATUE OF HENRY GRATTAN | BANK OF IRELAND |

ALLIED IRISH (FORMERLY ROYAL), BANK, FOSTER PLACE.

The building in Foster Place which now accommodates a branch of the Allied Irish Bank was originally designed by Charles Geoghegan as the head office of the Royal Bank which was founded in 1869. A branch of the bank was built at 63, Upper O'Connell Street in 1869.

The Bank of Ireland portico in Foster Place, opposite the present Allied Irish Bank, was designed by Robert Parke and built in 1797. The curved wall of the Bank of Ireland was designed by Francis Johnston.

The Armoury, Foster Place, designed by Francis Johnston, was built at the end of Foster Place about 1810. The carved feature by Thomas Kirk over the impressive front entrance gateway is a well-balanced composition consisting of items of artillery.

THE ARMOURY ANNEXE OR GUARD HOUSE, FOSTER PLACE.

BANK OF IRELAND, RATHMINES.

The Rathmines Branch of the Bank of Ireland was originally a branch of the National Bank, established in 1835. The red sandstone facade includes a carved pediment. There is a harp on the keystone over the left-hand ground floor window and a crown over the right-hand one. The tone of the facade harmonises with that of the Town Hall and other important buildings in the centre of Rathmines.

Before the public library building was erected at the corner of Leinster Road in 1913, the library was located at 67 Rathmines Road, and earlier still at 53 Rathmines Road, where it was set up in 1877.

The Carnegie Libraries at Ballyboden and Clondalkin were designed by T. J. Byrne, later Chief Architect, Office of Public Works.

The Trustee Savings Bank, 114-115 Lower Grafton Street, opposite the Provost's House in Trinity College, occupies the premises previously owned by the Northern Bank. This imposing four-storey building was designed by Lanyon, Lynn and Lanyon, who also designed St. Andrew's Church, St. Andrew Street; the Unitarian Church, St. Stephen's Green; and the Nineteenth-Century extension to St. Doulough's Church, Malahide.

On the left of the Trustee Savings Bank, the premises, 113 Grafton Street, also has an interesting and well-preserved facade.

TRUSTEE SAVINGS BANK,
114-115 LOWER GRAFTON STREET.

The Broadstone Railway Terminus designed in Egyptian style by John Skipton Mulvany was built in 1850 for the Midland Great Western Railway. The eastern colonnade was added in 1861. The railway line was closed down in 1931 but the building is still used for transport purposes.

Broadstone was originally the starting point of the Royal Canal and the railway line was laid parallel with the waterway which the MGWR purchased with this purpose in view. The canal declined in importance and was eventually closed down in 1961. Efforts are being made to open it up to traffic again.

The Harcourt Street Terminus was designed in the Classical manner by George Wilkinson and built in 1859 for the Dublin and South Eastern Railway. It was meticulously planned and detailed and forms a very pleasing architectural composition. In contrast with the Broadstone Terminus which occupies a commanding position the Harcourt Street building fits unobtrusively into the streetscape. The railway line was closed in 1958 and the station building was converted for use as offices.

HARCOURT
STREET
RAILWAY
TERMINUS
NOW
BARCLAY'S
BANK.

OFFICE
BLOCK,
HEUSTON
STATION.

The ornate administration block of Heuston (formerly Kingsbridge) Station, designed by Sancton Wood in the Italianate Renaissance style was built in 1845 for Great Southern and Western Railway. The long and comparatively low railway station has an arcaded entrance porch.

The redbrick Nurses' Home building, belonging to the former Dr. Steeven's Hospital, is on the opposite side of St. John's Road, on the corner of Steeven's Lane.

Connolly Station, Amiens Street, is illustrated on page 149.

HEUSTON
RAILWAY
STATION.

169

TOWN HALL, DÚN LAOGHAIRE.

The Venetian style Town Hall, Dún Laoghaire, designed by J. L. Robinson, was built in 1880. The building, with its 37 m high clock tower, occupies an important corner site near the railway station. It is faced in red and grey Scottish sandstone and features pierced balconies and arched windows. The interior is well preserved by the Borough Council.

Other work carried out by the architect J. L. Robinson in Dún Laoghaire include St. Michael's Hospital (1874) and the People's Park (1890). The Post Office, adjoining the Town Hall, was designed by E. T. Owen of the Office of Public Works and built in 1879.

Dún Laoghaire Railway Station, designed by John Skipton Mulvany, was built in 1842. A restaurant is now located in part of the building at street level.

RESTAURANT, NA MARA, DÚN LAOGHAIRE RAILWAY STATION.

LIGHTHOUSE
EAST PIER,
DÚN LAOGHAIRE.

At the beginning of the Nineteenth Century Dublin Bay was extremely dangerous for shipping. An Act of Parliament passed in 1815 gave powers for the erection of an asylum harbour and place of refuge in Dún Laoghaire.

The lighthouse and anenometer were erected by the middle of the century.

The coastguard houses in Dún Laoghaire, built in 1859, were designed by James Higgins Owen.

Mainly due to the efforts of a Norwegian, Captain Richard Toucher, the construction of the large refuge harbour in Dún Laoghaire was begun in 1817 but it was not completed until 1861. Granite from Dalkey, Glasthule and Dún Laoghaire was used in the work. A Scotsman, John Rennie, assisted by John Aird, was in charge of the project. In addition to the East and West Piers, the Traders Wharf and the Lighthouse were constructed. The mail packet service was switched from Howth to Dún Laoghaire in 1834 and the Carlisle Pier was constructed in 1859.

Unfortunately the decorative cast iron fountain near the Railway Station was destroyed by vandals in 1981. It was of a type produced by English ironworks.

IRON FOUNTAIN,
DÚN LAOGHAIRE.

ROYAL
IRISH
YACHT
CLUB,
DÚN
LAOGHAIRE.

The Royal Irish Yacht Club, Dún Laoghaire, designed by John Skipton Mulvany (pupil of William Deane Butler), was built in 1851. It is laid out on a symmetrical plan with the principal rooms overlooking the harbour. There are pavilions on each side of the impressive central colonnade.

The National Yacht Club, Dún Laoghaire, designed by William Sterling, was built adjacent to the East Pier in 1870. Constructed on a projecting granite base, a distinctive feature of the building are the three pediments which front the slated roofs.

NATIONAL
YACHT CLUB,
DÚN
LAOGHAIRE.

STATUE OF WILLIAM DARGAN, NATIONAL GALLERY OF IRELAND, MERRION SQUARE.

The bronze statue of William Dargan, who was responsible for the setting up of the Dublin to Dún Laoghaire railway and for the Great International Exhibition mounted by the Royal Dublin Society on Leinster Lawn in 1853, stands in front of the National Gallery of Ireland. It is very appropriate that the statue should be located here as Dargan donated a large sum of money to the art section of the Exhibition which resulted in the establishment of the National Gallery. The statue of Dargan is by Thomas Farrell.

Dargan lived in Mount Annville and in 1865 he signed over this property to the Sisters of the Sacred Heart who set up their school there.

The Royal George Yacht Club was designed by J. S. Mulvany.

ROYAL GEORGE YACHT CLUB, DÚN LAOGHAIRE.

MARTELLO TOWER,
SANDYMOUNT.

In the period 1804-15 a large number of Martello Towers were built along the east coast from Balbriggan to Bray as defence against a possible French invasion. The sloping walls of the round towers are almost 2.4 m thick and 12 m high. There is a gun platform on the roof behind the parapet wall in each case. Lt.-Col. Fisher was responsible for the design and construction of these massive granite buildings based on a tower in Martella, Corsica.

The Martello tower at Sandycove was occupied for a period by James Joyce and Oliver St. John Gogarty. It was purchased by the architect Michael Scott who was one of those responsible for the setting up of the Joyce Museum which was opened in the tower in 1962.

MARTELLO
TOWER,
SANDYCOVE.

174

BAILY
LIGHT-
HOUSE,
DUNGRIFFEN
PROMENTARY,
HOWTH.

The Baily Lighthouse, on the promentary below Howth Head, was built in 1814.

The lighthouse building could accommodate as many as thirty people but the lighthouse is now automated.

Throughout the Nineteenth Century and the early part of the Twentieth Century many developments took place on the lands close to the coastline from Howth on the northside to Killiney on the southside. Increasing numbers of houses were built according as transport facilities improved.

The main piers in Howth Harbour were completed in 1812 and the Mail Packet Station was moved from Ringsend. The harbour was taken in charge by the Office of Public Works in 1832.

The mail boat service between Howth and Holyhead was inaugurated in 1814 but it was transferred to Dún Laoghaire in 1836 after the opening of the railway service to the southern suburbs.

LIGHTHOUSE,
HOWTH HARBOUR.

175

IDA ENTERPRISE CENTRE, PEARSE STREET.

The IDA Enterprise Centre Building, Pearse Street, was originally a sugar refinery. It was designed by Alfred Darbyshire, an English architect, at the age of twenty-three. His consulting engineer was William Fairbairn, who pioneered the use of wrought-iron beams and brick arches to carry very heavy superimposed loads on the floors of this eight-storey building which was erected in 1862. The black limestone and granite walls have weathered well. Bewley Moss and Co. were the original owners of the building which was later used as a distillery warehouse. The Industrial Development Authority purchased the building from Hammond Lane Foundry.

The former C.I.É. Warehouse, North Wall, is to be converted into a concert hall. This extensive building with walls of stone and brick stands on a site of nearly three hectares and the proposed concert hall will accommodate several thousand spectators.

FORMER C.I.É. POINT DEPOT, NORTH WALL.

GAS HOLDER, SIR JOHN ROGERSON'S QUAY.

The huge gas holder which has occupied a very prominent position on the south quay since 1934 cannot be considered an attractive feature of the skyline.

The older gas holders, however, are set back further from the Liffey they are smaller in volume and much less obtrusive. The iron framework which surrounds one of them is both functional and decorative. It was supplied by Clayton & Sons, Leeds, in 1871.

GAS HOLDERS, SHELBOURNE ROAD, RINGSEND.

SEÁN
HEUSTON
BRIDGE,
FORMERLY
KING'S
BRIDGE.

Built in 1828, it was designed by George Papworth. Sarah Bridge, next up river, was built by Stevens in 1793.

This elliptical cast-iron bridge, aligned with Steeven's Lane on the south side of the Liffey, leads to Parkgate Street on the north side.

In 1982 Frank Sherwin Bridge, between Seán Heuston Bridge and Rory O'Moore Bridge, was opened.

RORY
O'MOORE
BRIDGE,
FORMERLY
VICTORIA
BRIDGE.

Built in
1863, it was
designed
by Robert
Daglish
Junior,
St. Helen's
Foundry,
Lancashire,
England.

This iron bridge crosses the Liffey between Watling Street on the south side of the river and Wolfe Tone Quay and Ellis Quay on the north side.

O'Donovan Rossa Bridge, formerly Richmond Bridge, was built in 1813 to replace an earlier bridge destroyed by flood waters. It is in line with Winetavern Street on the south side of the river and with Chancery Place on the north side. There are carved stones in the arches on both sides of the bridge.

O'DONOVAN
ROSSA
BRIDGE,
FORMERLY
RICHMOND
BRIDGE.

GRATTAN
BRIDGE,
FORMERLY
ESSEX
BRIDGE.

Grattan Bridge, formerly known as Essex Bridge, was designed by John Semple. It connects Parliament Street and Capel Street. The bridge was built in 1775 but was rebuilt by the Dublin Port and Docks Board in 1875 when it was given its new name by the Municipal Council. The engineer was Bindon B. Stoney.

O'CONNELL
BRIDGE,
FORMERLY
CARLISLE
BRIDGE.

Carlisle Bridge, designed by James Gandon, was erected in 1784. This comparatively narrow humped bridge was replaced by the present bridge, named O'Connell Bridge, in 1880.

The Whitworth Bridge was built in 1813 and a new balustrade constructed in 1890. The bridge, renamed Fr. Mathew Bridge in 1938, is aligned with Bridge Street and Church Street.

FATHER
MATHEW
BRIDGE.

HUBAND BRIDGE, HERBERT PLACE.

The hump-backed Huband Bridge, built in 1791, spans the Grand Canal in the vicinity of Herbert Place, Warrington Place and Percy Place.

In the Nineteenth Century and the early part of the Twentieth Century large quantities of food and fuel were transported to the city on the canals which were navigable for boats up to 60 tons. It was an economical form of transport which ensured that farm produce from the midlands could be made available at reasonable prices in the Dublin markets.

Work on the Grand Canal was commenced in 1756 under the direction of Thomas Omer, engineer of the Board of Inland Navigation. In spite of technical and financial difficulties the work was completed by 1791. Construction of the Royal Canal on the north side of the city was completed in 1789 with the opening of Broadstone Harbour. Passenger traffic was discontinued in 1858.

Mount Street Bridge, a short distance from Huband Bridge, is another of the numerous stone bridges which replaced the earlier wooden canal bridges.

MOUNT STREET BRIDGE OVER THE GRAND CANAL.

BRIDGE OVER THE RIVER DODDER AT TEMPLEOGUE.

The triple-arched stone bridge over the Dodder at Templeogue served its purpose well until greatly increased volume of traffic rendered it necessary to widen the road and to form the present Austin Clarke Bridge.

A short distance up the river at Firhouse a weir was constructed in the Thirteenth Century to divert water from the Dodder to the city supply. This arrangement was continued until the supply was superseded by the high-pressure Vartry system from Co. Wicklow which was laid on in 1868.

The first stone bridge over the river Dodder in Ringsend was constructed in 1803 to replace an earlier timber one damaged by flood waters.

London Bridge, Irishtown, was rebuilt in 1856. Ball's Bridge, first erected in 1751 was rebuilt in 1791, rebuilt for the second time in 1832. Waldron's Bridge, Orwell Road, was built in 1848.

Other bridges built over the Dodder include those at Clonskeagh, Milltown and Rathfarnham.

BRIDGE OVER THE RIVER DODDER AT RINGSEND.

A spectacular international exhibition was mounted in Herbert Park in 1907. Many buildings were specially constructed for the occasion, including a Somali village. The pergola is one feature which has survived.

The People's Park, Dún Laoghaire, was laid out by J. L. Robinson, architect, in 1890.

The Zoological Gardens in the Phoenix Park were opened in 1818. It was one of the first public zoos in the world. The Tudor style gate house was built in 1832.

The Tudor style gate house was built in 1832.

ZOO,
PHOENIX
PARK.

ST. STEPHEN'S
GREEN.

Lord
Ardilaun
of Ashford
enhanced
St. Stephen's
Green and
handed
it over to
the public
in 1877.
A statue
of the
benefactor
was
erected
in the
Green
in 1882.

After St. Stephen's Green was handed over to the residents of the Square in 1814, at a nominal rent, the amenity was developed by improving the drainage and planting trees, shrubs and flowers, enclosing the gardens and providing perimeter lighting. Lord Ardilaun, Sir Arthur Guinness, purchased the park in 1876. The park was laid out at his expense and it was opened to the public in 1880. Since then the citizens of Dublin and visitors to the capital have enjoyed the pleasures of the attractively laid-out park with its artificial lake, bridges, fountains, bandstand and numerous monuments. It covers an area of approximately 11 hectares.

PALMERS-
TOWN
PARK.

HOUSES, HARCOURT TERRACE.

A number of Regency style houses, built about 1840, form an interesting and attractive streetscape on one side of Harcourt Terrace.

Block 6/7 has a large-scale order executed in stucco and surmounted by a Greek-style frieze.

No. 4, on the right-hand side of the pair illustrated below, was the home of the theatrical personalities, Micheál Mac Liammóir and Hilton Edwards.

Regency type terraced houses can be seen in Upper Leeson Street, Dún Laoghaire and Monkstown.

HOUSES, HARCOURT TERRACE.

MOUNT PLEASANT SQUARE, RANELAGH.

Mount Pleasant Square, Ranelagh, was built in 1830-40.

Leinster Square, Rathmines, was built about the same period but Belgrave Square, Rathmines, was built somewhat later.

George Bernard Shaw was born at No. 33, Synge Street , in 1856.

33, SYNGE STREET, BIRTHPLACE OF GEORGE BERNARD SHAW.

END-OF-TERRACE HOUSE
AT JUNCTION OF
WATERLOO ROAD AND
BURLINGTON ROAD.

In the Nineteenth Century houses were commonly built in terraces but special treatment was given to many end houses, as in the case of this one at the junction of Waterloo Road and Burlington Road, where space permitted the building of a projecting entrance block.

Highfield Road was first opened up in 1756, thus connecting Rathmines and Rathgar. Rathgar Road was not opened up until 1815. Both roads have a mixture of detached, semi-detached and terraced houses. Down through the years spaces between the houses have been filled in and additions made to the accommodation in existing houses.

END-OF-TERRACE HOUSE,
HIGHFIELD ROAD,
RATHGAR.

TERRACE HOUSE, WATERLOO ROAD.

Waterloo Road and Wellington Road were opened up in 1846 and building of houses on these wide thoroughfares was commenced. Building was also started on the south side of Pembroke Road. Morehampton Road and Lansdowne Road, too, were developed in the middle of the Nineteenth Century. The two-storey house with basement, as seen in Waterloo Road, is typical of the design said to have been originated by George Papworth.

Many other new roads were developed in the vicinity of Ballsbridge in the first half of the Nineteenth Century. Northumberland Road was first opened. up in 1832 but houses had already been built in Upper Baggot Street and in Pembroke Road.

LARGE SEMI-DETACHED HOUSES, LANSDOWNE ROAD.

This terrace of houses at Wilton Place faces onto an attractive little park. The stone facing to the bottom storey and the stone quoins contrast with the brick facing of the upper storeys. The front wall is capped with a stone cornice and there are wrought-iron balconies at the first- and second-floor levels. There is a balustrade to the basement area instead of the more usual wrought iron railings.

The canal-side buildings from Wilton Place to Baggot Street were in descending scale but the two-storey buildings shown here have been replaced by comparatively tall office blocks.

The church which occupied a low-level site around the corner in Baggot Street has also been replaced by an office block.

CANAL-SIDE BUILDINGS,
NEAR BAGGOT STREET BRIDGE.

TERRACE
OF
HOUSES,
LOWER
BAGGOT
STREET.

A unified architectural effect was achieved in the building of even very long thoroughfares such as Baggot Street and monotony was avoided by subtle differences in the design of individual houses. In spite of developments in the Twentieth Century, parts of Baggot Street still retain much of their original character.

The houses in the nearby Fitzwilliam Square, built in the first decade of the Nineteenth Century, are well preserved in spite of changes in use from residential to professional and commercial use.

PAIR OF
HOUSES,
LOWER
BAGGOT
STREET.

HOUSES,
MOUNTJOY
SQUARE.

Mountjoy Square was not completed until about 1818 but by then the speculative building boom, which Dublin had experienced during the latter half of the Eighteenth Century, was waning. Some of the larger houses became vacant. As time went on houses were subdivided and let out to tenants but unfortunately some owners neglected to maintain their premises in proper condition.

Other developments nearing completion at the turn of the century included Temple Street, Denmark Street, Great Charles Street and Gardiner Place – Luke Gardiner's proposed Circus at the junction of Eccles Street and Berkley Street never materialised.

MOUNTJOY
SQUARE.

PEMBROKE
STREET WEST.

Pembroke Street West connects Lower Leeson Street and Fitzwilliam Square. The tall terraced houses, four storeys above basement, contrast with the detatched houses set in large gardens, which can be seen in Upper Leeson Street and its vicinity, only a short distance away.

In Wellington Place, off Upper Leeson Street, there is a mixture of house styles. Some of the houses are detached, some are semi-detached, or terraced, some are tall, others quite low.

DETACHED
HOUSE,
WELLINGTON
PLACE

TERRACED HOUSES,
WARRINGTON PLACE.

Herbert Place, Herbert Street and other streets in the same vicinity were developed towards the middle of the Nineteenth Century.

The influence of the style of domestic architecture developed in the Eighteenth Century persisted throughout the Nineteenth Century, although the details were modified as time went on.

Many of the houses along Rathmines Road have been hidden by later shop buildings but some still retain their front gardens.

TERRACED HOUSES,
RATHMINES ROAD.

HEAD
GARDENER'S
HOUSE,
ST. STEPHEN'S
GREEN.

At the beginning of the Nineteenth Century St. Stephen's Green was in very poor condition. The maintenance of the park was then handed over to Commissioners representing the local residents. The gardens were tidied up and wrought iron gates and railings erected. Bollards and chains (the latter since removed) were put up along the outside of the footpaths. Arthur Guinness, Lord Ardilaun, converted the Green into an attractive park at his own expense and it was first opened to the public in general in 1880.

WELL-MAINTAINED COTTAGE STYLE HOUSE, TERENURE.

SHOP AND RESIDENCE, ST. STEPHEN'S GREEN.

In the Nineteenth Century the buildings around St. Stephen's Green gradually lost their residential character as demand for professional accommodation increased. Shops became a growing feature on the north and west sides. Residential accommodation on the upper floors was converted to office use.

The building on the right above was the last private residence on St. Stephen's Green. It is now used for commercial purposes.

Doran's barber shop in Rathmines is an example of urban vernacular architecture which is common in many parts of the city. In Rathmines and elsewhere shops were built in front of private houses without much consideration for the streetscape.

BARBER'S SHOP AND RESIDENCE, CASTLEWOOD AVENUE, RANELAGH.

HOUSE AT
CORNER OF
NORTHBROOK
ROAD AND
LEESON
STREET.

A comparatively low double-fronted house was constructed in Northbrook Road, an unusual treatment at the gable end of a high terrace of houses in Upper Leeson Street. Maximum use was made of the limited space available.

There is no special treatment at the end of the terrace of double-fronted houses in Charleston Road, Ranelagh. The two houses nearest the corner of Mountpleasant Avenue are rendered and painted.

The former Methodist Church on the opposite side of Charleston Road at the corner of Charleston Avenue, has been renovated and converted into office accommodation. Trinity House, as it is now called, was the subject of an environmental award made by Dublin Corporation.

DOUBLE FRONTED TERRACED HOUSES, CHARLESTON ROAD, RANELAGH.

FORMER
APOSTOLIC
NUNCIATURE,
PHOENIX PARK.

The former Apostolic Nunciature in the Phoenix Park was previously the Under Secretary's residence which incorporated a late medieval castle and an Eighteenth Century house. Conservatories were added in the Nineteenth Century at a time when other alterations were being made. On adaptation to the needs of the Nunciature the butler's room was converted into a chapel.

The building is located on the opposite side of the road to the American Ambassador's residence, formerly the Chief Secretary's Lodge built by Sir John de Blacquire.

Many of the large detached houses built in the Nineteenth Century and in the first decade of the Twentieth Century were planned with the main reception rooms on each side of a central entrance hall and two or three front bedrooms on the first floor. The fenestration commonly consisted of two windows below and three above but nevertheless there was considerable variety in the elevational treatment. Projecting porches were a popular feature and, where not provided originally, were in many cases added at a later date. Similarly, in some cases balustrades were part of the original design but in many other cases were a later addition. Many brick facades were rendered and various embellishments made in the process.

NEWTOWN
HOUSE,
BLACKROCK.

RATHFARNHAM CASTLE   Work by William Chambers and other architects.

The property which has become known as Rathfarnham Castle is in fact a composite structure erected over a period of centuries and including a Sixteenth-Century Castle. Some very fine interior decoration was carried out in the building in the Eighteenth Century under the direction of the architect William Chambers. Both he and James Stuart were responsible for some very fine ceilings, Angelica Kaufmann for an interesting picture painted in 1771. In the first half of the Nineteenth Century new developments posed a serious threat to the future of Rathfarnham Castle but alterations and extensive additions insured that the property was adapted to meet the requirements of the Society of Jesus who purchased the property in 1913. In 1985 the Jesuits, having sold the property, left Rathfarnham.

Although most of the original demesne has now been built upon, Rathfarnham Castle and its immediate surroundings are now the property of the State and could, with enlightened guidance, be put to good practical use compatible with their status as a national monument.

At the end of the Eighteenth Century the La Touche banking family acquired the Grange, Rathfarnham, and carried out extensive alterations and additions to the house which was renamed Marlay House. In 1864 the house was purchased by Robert Tedcastle of the coal merchant family. He sold part of the estate and on it Marlay Grange was built. The Grange Golf Club, laid out in 1910, included part of the former Grange property.

The Marlay Estate was bought by Dublin County Council in 1972 and three years later it was opened as a public park. The courtyard outbuildings have been developed as a craft centre.

MARLAY
HOUSE,
RATHFARNHAM.
REAR VIEW.

197

In 1870, Artane House, which occupies the site of a demolished castle, came into the possession of the Christian Brothers who established an industrial school there. The school was extended over the years to provide accommodation and training for a very large number of boys.

Sybil Hill, originally the dower house of the Ardilaun family, was purchased by the Vincentian Fathers who later built St. Paul's College on the grounds.

The O'Brien Institute, Malahide Road, designed by J. J. O'Callaghan and built in 1882, is a rather strident red brick building located near the beautiful Casino. The Institute building is now the property of Dublin Corporation where it has located a training centre for the Fire Service.

O'BRIEN INSTITUTE, MALAHIDE ROAD.

MOUNT
TEMPLE
SCHOOL,
MALAHIDE
ROAD.

Mount Temple, on the Bradshaw Estate, was built in 1862. Mountjoy School was transferred here in 1949 and a large Comprehensive School complex now surrounds the original building.

In the same way the original dwelling house at St. Columba's College, Rathfarnham, is surrounded by a large number of buildings in different styles, some built in the Nineteenth Century, others built in the Twentieth Century. St. Columba's College moved to Rathfarnham in 1849.

The High School, built in Harcourt Street in 1870, was demolished after the school moved to Rathgar in 1971. The Garda Síochána Headquarters now occupies the site of the red brick school buildings and playground.

Wesley College, founded at St. Stephen's Green in 1845, moved to Ballinteer in 1969 and the original school buildings were demolished to make way for offices.

The rows of brick-fronted houses which accommodated Alexandra College in Earlsfort Terrace were demolished after the girls' school moved to Milltown in 1972.

HOLLY PARK
HOUSE,
now the
Warden's
residence
ST. COLUMBA'S
COLLEGE,
RATHFARNHAM.

199

CHRISTIAN BROTHERS' SCHOOL, SYNGE STREET.

The granite-faced monastery and primary school and the brick-faced buildings at the rear are the oldest part of the Christian Brothers' Schools, Synge Street, which was founded in 1864. Down through the years many adjacent properties were acquired to meet the growing needs of the school and eventually new buildings were erected but the monastery and primary school have been retained.

Daniel O'Connell laid the foundation stone of the Catholic Model School, later named O'Connell School and sometimes referred to as Richmond Street School, in 1828. The foundation stone of the monastery was also laid the same year. The Christian Brothers took up residence in 1831 and the school was opened, replacing an earlier one in Jervis Street. The houses in North Richmond Street were built about the same time as the original school which was subsequently extended many times. The north wing was built in 1865 and a third storey was added in 1904.

At first the school was outside the city boundary but the city limits were extended in 1840 and again in 1900.

O'CONNELL SCHOOL, NORTH RICHMOND STREET.

ST. GABRIEL'S
NATIONAL SCHOOL,
COWPER STREET,
OFF AUGHRIM
STREET.

St. Gabriel's National School, Cowper Street, built in 1895, was extended and renovated in 1953. It has contrasting colours of brickwork and other decorative features. The older part of the school, with its lofty rooms and tall Gothic windows is a striking contrast.

The Christian Brothers' School in North Brunswick Street was established in 1869 when the only other schools in the vicinity were the one in Queen Street and the Girls' School in North King Street.

ST. GABRIEL'S
NATIONAL
SCHOOL
COWPER
STREET,
OFF AUGHRIM
STREET.

FORMER ST. STEPHEN'S SCHOOL, NORTHUMBERLAND ROAD.

When St. Stephen's school building located on Northumbrland Road near Mount Street Bridge, was no longer required for its original use it was put to new use as a training centre for the City of Dublin Vocational Education Committee.

Unfortunately many other valuable buildings have been demolished rather than adapting them to new use. For example, architecturally significant buildings in Molesworth Street were demolished to make way for new offices. These were St. Ann's Parochial Schools (1857) and Hall designed in the Gothic style by Deane and Woodward and a Neo-Classical house built in the 1830s.

ST. ANN'S PAROCHIAL SCHOOLS AND HALL MOLES-WORTH STREET.

LORETO ABBEY, RATHFARNHAM.

The focal point of the Loreto Abbey convent school complex is the Eighteenth-Century residence built by William Pallister but later occupied by John Grierson, King's Painter. The Institute of the Blessed Virgin Mary set up their mother house here in 1822.

The same order of nuns set up a convent and school at Bullough Castle in 1838.

ST. JAMES'S CATHOLIC CHURCH, JAMES'S STREET.

The Catholic Parish of St. James was constituted from St. Catherine's in 1724. The first stone of the Gothic Church of St. James, designed by Patrick Byrne, was laid by Daniel O'Connell in 1844 and the finished building was solemnly dedicated by Dr. Cullen in 1854.

The Gothic facade of the Church of SS. Michael and John, built in 1815, was designed by J. Taylor. The Smock Alley Theatre previously occupied the site in Exchange Street.

SS. MICHAEL AND JOHN'S CHURCH, EXCHANGE STREET.

CHRIST CHURCH AND SYNOD HALL

The original Christ Church Cathedral was completed in the first half of the Thirteenth Century and a choir added in the Fourteenth Century. The building was restored in 1871-78 by the noted English architect George Edmund Street, with the financial support of the distiller, Henry Roe. In the course of his work Street had the Fourteenth-Century Romanesque choir removed. The nave retains its Early Gothic character.

In 1841 the early Nineteenth-Century Church of St. Michael, designed by Edward Parke, was converted into the Synod Hall and connected to the Cathedral by means of an enclosed foot-bridge. The Synod Hall is now put to other uses.

CHRIST
CHURCH
CATHEDRAL

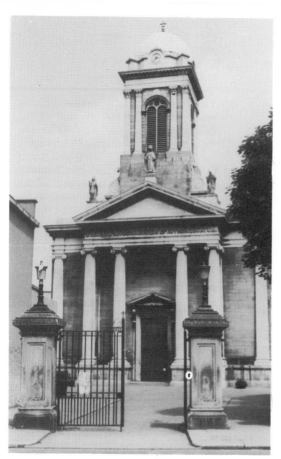

CHURCH OF ST. NICHOLAS OF MYRA, FRANCIS STREET

The Church of St. Nicholas of Myra, Francis Street, designed by John Leeson, was commenced in 1829, opened in 1834 and dedicated in 1856. The plan is in the form of a Greek cross. The Ionic portico, pediment, bell tower and cupola are later additions designed by Patrick Byrne and built about 1860. Inside there are gesso images and reliefs by the Irish artists John Hogan and Edward Smyth.

The Church of Our Lady of Refuge, Rathmines, designed by Patrick Byrne, was built in 1854. The architect, W. H. Byrne, later added a portico and pediment surmounted by statutes of the Blessed Virgin, St. Peter and St. Patrick. The church was restored after a fire in 1922. The opportunity was taken to enlarge the copper-covered dome.

St. Mary's College, on the opposite side of Rathmines Road, was founded in 1890.

The statue of Our Lady of Refuge, on the apex of the pediment is by James Farrell.

CHURCH OF OUR LADY OF REFUGE, RATHMINES.

ST. STEPHEN'S CHURCH, MOUNT STREET CRESCENT.

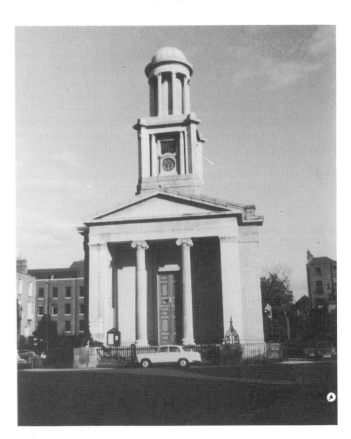

St. Stephen's Church, Mount Street Crescent, popularly known as the Pepper Canister, was designed by John Bowden and completed about 1827 by John Welland. The late Classical building very effectively closes the vista at the end of Upper Mount Street. It can be seen from Merrion Square, from Herbert Street and from Huband Bridge, situated as the church is in the middle of a Nineteenth Century crescent.

Herbert Street was built about 1830.

ST. STEPHEN'S CHURCH, CLOSING THE VISTA AT THE END OF UPPER MOUNT ST.

ST. PAUL'S, ARRAN QUAY.

St. Paul's Church, Arran Quay (1835-37), designed by Patrick Byrne, was solemnly opened in 1837. The portico (without statues), bell turret and cupola were added in 1842. The bells, made by James Sheridan of Church Street, were swung into position in 1843. It has a simple nave and apse and externally a prostyle Ionic portico with classical pediment.

The same architect designed the portico of St. Audoen's, High Street. He also designed Adam and Eve's, Merchants' Quay; St. Joseph's, Terenure; and St. Patrick's, Glencullen.

The parochial house adjoining St. Paul's, Arran Quay, was built in 1923.

Another architect, John Burke, also did work at St. Paul's. Other buildings with which he was associated include the Church of the Immaculate Conception, Inchicore; Clonliffe Diocesan Seminary and the Mater Misericordiae Hospital, Eccles Street.

St. Paul's with its bell tower and cupola, adds distinction to the Liffey-side scene in the vicinity of Arran Quay.

ST. PAUL'S, ARRAN QUAY.

ST. GEORGE'S CHURCH, HARDWICKE PLACE.

St. George's Church (1802-13), designed by Francis Johnston, resembles some of the London churches designed by Christopher Wren. A fine example of the Renaissance style, it has an imposing prostyle Greek classical portico constructed of Portland stone. The frieze above the fluted Ionic columns carries a Greek inscription and there are carved heads on the keystones.

The nearby Children's Hospital in Temple Street was originally founded as St. Joseph's Infirmary in 1876.

The graceful four-storey steeple of St. George's Church, rising to a height of 60 m, is an attractive feature of the north city scene while the building as a whole closes the vista at the end of Hardwicke Street.

Francis Johnston, architect of St. George's, also designed the Early Gothic Chapel Royal (1814), now the Church of the Most Holy Trinity, in Dublin Castle. There is a striking contrast of styles between the two churches.

STEEPLE,
ST. GEORGE'S CHURCH,
HARDWICKE PLACE.

THE OLD
ST. AUDOEN'S CHURCH,
HIGH STREET.

The old St. Audoen's Church, High Street, adjacent to the remains of the City Wall, has a very long history stretching back many centuries. The precincts have undergone some changes in the Eighteenth and Nineteenth Centuries but the church and stone tower have been well preserved and their appearance has been enhanced by the small park which has been attractively laid out by Dublin Corporation.

Another well-known landmark in the Liberties is located in Watling Street, off Thomas Street West.

This copper-capped brick tower (c. 1800) was originally a windmill owned by Roe's distillery. The 45 m high structure was later incorporated in the Guinness's brewery complex set up in James's Street in 1759. The figure on top of the dome is that of St. Patrick.

The Hop Stone in Rainsford Street, built in the last quarter of the Nineteenth Century, has been converted into an Exhibition Centre. The exterior is faced with local brick; the spacious interior has timber floors supported on cast iron columns.

TOWER,
WATLING STREET.

ST. AUDOEN'S, HIGH STREET.

St. Audoen's Church (1841-47) was designed by Patrick Byrne. The dome collapsed in the 1880s and it was never replaced. The portico, designed by Stephen Ashlin and Patrick Byrne, was added in 1898.

The neo-classical interior has fluted Corinthian pilasters, cornice and high-level windows. The coffered ceiling is barrel vaulted.

St. Andrew's Church, Westland Row, designed by John Boulger, was completed in 1837. There is a Doric portico with a statue of St. Andrew above the pediment. The copper-topped tower is not visible from Westland Row. The side walls are of black Dublin calp.

Inside four tall scaglio columns support the baldachino. There is a sculpture of the Ascension by John Hogan and in the mortuary chapel a Madonna by William Pearse.

ST. ANDREW'S CHURCH, WESTLAND ROW.

ABBEY PRESBYTERIAN CHURCH, PARNELL SQUARE

The Abbey Church (1864), Parnell Square, was designed in the Gothic style by Andrew Heiton. The building of the church was financed by a wealthy Dublin merchant, Alex Findlater, and as a result it has become popularly known as Findlater's Church.

Parnell (formerly Rutland) Square and Cavendish Row were designed by John Ensor.

Findlater's Church, with its tall spire, occupies a commanding site at the corner of Parnell Square and North Frederick Street which was laid out in 1795. The Abbey Church contrasts with the earlier Presbyterian Church in Seán McDermott Street (formerly Gloucester Street) which was built in the Greek style in 1835.

There is a Presbyterian Church (known as the Scots Church) in Lower Abbey Street. The one in Ormond Quay was demolished.

REPAIRING THE SPIRE OF THE ABBEY PRESBYTERIAN CHURCH.

212

ST. PETER'S CHURCH, PHIBSBORO.

The building of the first church at the junction of Cabra Road and North Circular Road was commenced in 1823. The Vincentians moved into Phibsboro in 1838 at a time when there was only a small population of poor people living in simple cabins at the junction of four parishes. The Congregation of the Missions built the present enlarged church in the period 1902-11. The eastern end was designed by Goldie, Childe and Goldie and the nave was designed by Ashlin and Coleman. Hadfield was another architect who carried out work for the church.

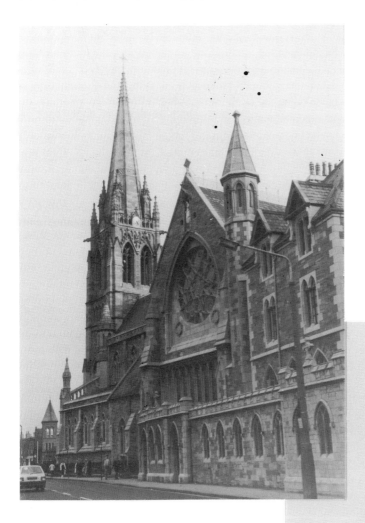

The small brick church, seen here to the left of St. Peter's, is Phibsboro Baptist Church.

St. Jude's Church, Inchicore, has been demolished with the exception of the tower and spire, which are being preserved to form part of a new development.

Materials from the demolished part were taken away for use in a new building in Straffan, Co. Kildare.

St. Michael's Catholic Church, Inchicore, was previously the garrison church of the Richmond Infirmary Barracks, built in 1807.

FORMER ST. JUDE'S CHURCH, INCHICORE.

ST. PATRICK'S, RINGSEND.

St. Patrick's Church, Ringsend, was built in 1912, replacing an earlier one dating from 1859. Externally the clock tower and spire are attractive features of the church which is sited on the bank of the Dodder and internally the windows display some good examples of Dublin stained glass.

The South Wall was completed before the end of the Eighteenth Century and the Pigeon House Fort was built in 1814.

The Church of Our Lady, Star of the Sea, Sandymount, was dedicated in 1853. It was designed by J. J. McCarthy in the medieval Gothic style, with gabled roofs to the nave and aisles. The proposed spire was never built but side porches were added in 1882. The walls are of Dublin granite with an elaborate main entrance doorway.

A boys school was built beside the Star of the Sea Church in the 1870s. Girls had already been provided for at the nearby Lakelands Convent.

CHURCH OF
OUR LADY,
STAR OF
THE SEA,
SANDYMOUNT.

SPIRE, ST. MICHAEL'S CHURCH, DÚN LAOGHAIRE.

St. Michael's Church, Dún Laoghaire, built in 1894, was designed by J. J. McCarthy, who also designed the Church of Our Lady, Star of the Sea, Sandymount; St. Patrick and St. Paul of the Cross, Mount Argus, Harold's Cross; and St. Mary of the Angels, Church Street. The church in Dún Laoghaire was destroyed by fire in 1965 but the tower and spire escaped damage and these are now incorporated in the new church.

The Mariners' Church, Haigh Terrace, built in 1837 and reconstructed in 1867, now houses the National Maritime Museum. Application was made to the Harbour Commissioners for a site near the harbour on the grounds that the church would be of particular benefit to visiting sailors.

The Harbour Master, William Hutchinson, was involved in the negotiations which led to acquisition of the site.

FORMER
MARINERS' CHURCH,
NOW THE
MARITIME MUSEUM,
DÚN LAOGHAIRE.

UNITARIAN CHURCH, ST. STEPHEN'S GREEN.

The Decorated Gothic style Unitarian Church, schools and ancillary accommodation on St. Stephen's Green were designed by William H. Lynn of Lanyon, Lynn and Lanyon, Belfast, and built in 1863. The spire is slated and the walls are faced with granite. The present Damer Hall is part of the former school.

Most of the buildings on this side of St. Stephen's Green, between Cuffe Street and York Street, have been replaced by modern office blocks.

William H. Lynn of Lanyon, Lynn and Lanyon also designed St. Andrew's Church located where Suffolk Street and St. Andrew's Street meet. The building closes the vista at the end of the narrow Church Lane. The Gothic steeple is a particularly attractive feature and there is a statue of St. Andrew by Edward Smyth. W. H. Lynn's appointment as architect to design the church was as a result of a competition. It was opened in 1862, replacing an earlier one which had been destroyed by fire. Raffles Brown was the architect commissioned to complete the work.

On the left-hand side of the Lane is the Northern Bank.

ST. ANDREW'S,
SUFFOLK STREET/
ST. ANDREW STREET,
AS SEEN FROM
CHURCH LANE.

ST. KEVIN'S CHURCH, HARRINGTON STREET.

The parish of St. Kevin was constituted in 1855 from Francis Street, designed by George Ashlin. Other churches designed by the same architect include those in Inchicore, Rathfarnham and Tallaght. He was also responsible for some of the work carried out at St. Peter's, Phibsboro.

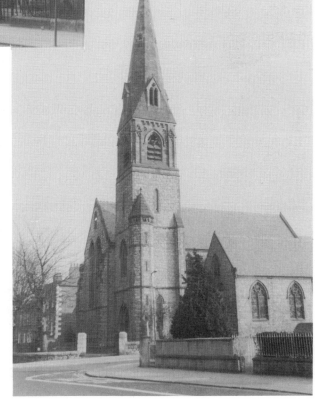

St. Kevin's Church of Ireland, South Circular Road, designed by Thomas Drew, was built in 1887-89. It is faced externally with Wicklow granite and Dumfries red sandstone and internally with Bath stone to columns and arches. Carving was executed by Harrison of North Brunswick Street, now Pearse Street. The nave is 24 m x 7.6 m and the height of the tower is 46 m to the weather vane. St. Kevin's Parochial Hall was designed by Rawson Carroll and Bachelor. It too is built with granite and Dumfries red sandstone.

FORMER ST. KEVIN'S
CHURCH OF IRELAND,
SOUTH CIRCULAR ROAD.

ST. JOSEPH'S CHURCH, TERENURE.

St. Joseph's Church, Terenure, designed by W. H. Byrne, was dedicated in 1904. It is faced externally with Wicklow granite and inside there are columns of Aberdeen granite. The gates and railings were erected in 1916. There are fine stained glass windows by Harry Clarke which were put in position in 1920. The church has been extended to twice its original size.

St. Joseph's Schools and the Presentation Convent were founded in 1866.

Christ Church, Leeson Park, now accommodates not only the congregation of the Leeson Park Parish of the Church of Ireland but also that of the Methodist Centenary Church, St. Stephen's Green. Christ Church and the adjoining asylum were designed by Rawson Carroll, architect, following a competition held in 1859.

CHRIST CHURCH, LEESON PARK.

HOLY TRINITY CHURCH, CHURCH AVENUE, RATHMINES.

The Church of the Holy Trinity, designed by John Semple, was built in 1828 for the members of the Church of Ireland residing in the growing new suburb of Rathmines. The Gothic style church is located in the middle of the road where Church Avenue and Belgrave Road meet.

Upper Rathmines Road and Palmerston Road were being developed at the time Holy Trinity Church was built.

On Sandford Road, not very far from Holy Trinity Church, in 1828 the Church of Ireland built Sandford Church facing Marlboro Road. In 1858 the church was extended and a new facade built to the design of Lanyon and Lynn, architects.

Beside the Church are Sandford Parish National School and Sandford Park School.

The Jesuits moved into Milltown Park in 1859 and established their Scholasticate and Retreat House there.

The Carmelites had moved into Ranelagh in the early part of the Nineteenth Century.

CHURCH OF IRELAND, SANDFORD ROAD, RANELAGH.

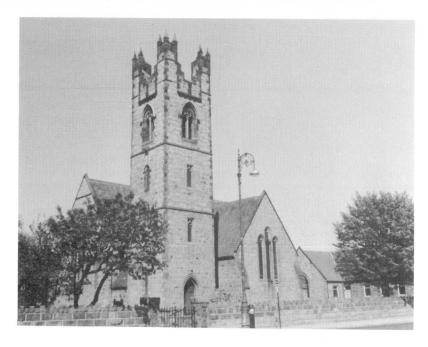

PRESBYTERIAN
CHURCH,
CLONTARF.

The walls are of
granite with red
sandstone quoins
and dressings,
creating a
polychromatic
effect. The tall
tower with cor-
ner pinnacles is a
striking feature,
located as it is at
the junction of
two important
roads.

The Presbyterian Church at the junction of the Howth and Clontarf roads was designed by Sir Thomas Drew and officially opened in 1890. The tower was added later. A special feature of the granite-faced building is a stained-glass window by Harry Clarke.

The nearby double-arched skew bridge was designed by Sir John O'Neill.

The Howth Road School was commenced in 1892, extended in 1910 and again in 1951.

The single storey
school building,
facing Clontarf,
harmonises with
the adjacent
church.

SCHOOL,
CLONTARF
ROAD,
ADJACENT TO
PRESBYTERIAN
CHURCH.

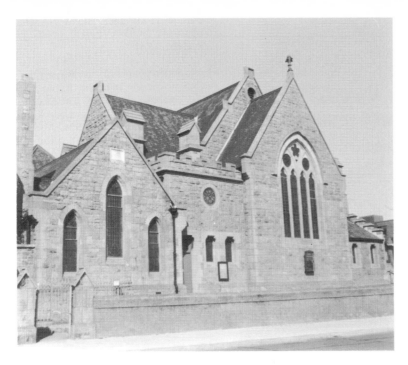

The first Methodist church in Clontarf was built at the corner of St. Lawrence's Road in 1867. It was renovated and enlarged in 1881 and replaced by the present granite-faced building, designed by Millar and Symes, built in 1906.

Other Methodist churches are in Sutton, Rathmines and Rathgar.

The Bull Wall and bridge were built about 1820.

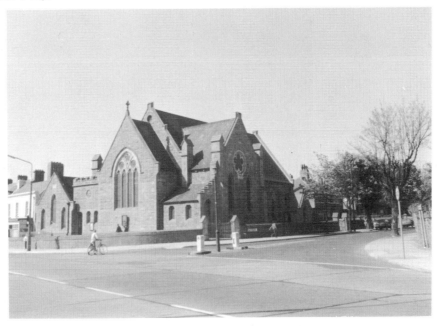

METHODIST
CHURCH,
CLONTARF.

221

CHURCH OF THE HOLY NAME, BEECHWOOD AVENUE, RANELAGH.

A wooden chapel-of-ease was erected in Cullenswood in 1898 and the new parish was established in 1906. The Church of the Holy Name, Beechwood Avenue, Ranelagh, was built in 1908. A striking feature is the tall Gothic bell tower.

Highfield Road was laid out in the first quarter of the Nineteenth Century and Rathgar Road was laid our in the middle of the century.

The Presbyterian Church, Rathgar, stands in a commanding position at the junction of Highfield Road and Rathgar Road. In all four churches were built in Rathgar about 1862.

PRESBYTERIAN
CHRIST CHURCH,
RATHGAR.

CHURCH OF THE THREE PATRONS, RATHGAR.

The foundation stone of the Church of the Three Patrons, Rathgar, was laid in 1881. It was opened the following year when Rathgar became a separate parish. The plain facade, designed by W. H. Byrne, was erected in 1894. Inside the church a special feature is the ambulatory around the nave and chancel.

Rathgar Road dates from the early part of the Nineteenth Century. Nos. 49 and 50 were acquired for use as presbyteries.

The Diocesan Seminary, Holy Cross Chapel, Clonliffe, was opened by Cardinal Cullen in 1860 and extensive buildings were later erected on the lands of Clonliffe House. The chapel, designed by John Bourke, was dedicated in 1876.

In 1890 the Archbishop of Dublin, Dr. Walsh, moved from Rutland (now Parnell) Square to the spacious house built in the grounds of Clonliffe College at Drumcondra Road.

CHAPEL OF THE HOLY CROSS, CLONLIFFE COLLEGE, CLONLIFFE ROAD.

CHURCH OF ST. JOHN THE BAPTIST, CLONTARF.

The first Catholic church of St. John the Baptist in Clontarf was opened in 1825. The second one, designed by Patrick Byrne, was opened in 1895. It is located in a prominent position at the corner of Vernon Avenue and Clontarf Road.

The separate parish of Clontarf was formed in 1829. The parish was later divided up, forming new parishes in Raheny and Coolock.

The Protestant Church of St. John the Baptist, Seafield Road, off Castle Avenue, was designed by Welland and Gillespie, and opened in 1866. A granite-faced building, it has a 45 m spire.

In 1847 the site was secured for the Catholic church in Fairview. The Church of the Visitation, built in 1855, replaced an earlier parochial chapel. The church was extended in the early years of the Twentieth Century.

The former Town Hall in Clontarf was converted into St. Anthony's Church. The extensions and alterations were carried out under the direciton of John J. Robinson, architect, in 1927. A new church was built at the rear in 1975 and the old building is once again in use as a hall.

The former Town Hall in Clontarf was converted into St. Anthony's Church. The extensions and alterations were carried out under the direction of John J. Robinson, architect, in 1927. A new church was built at the rear in 1975 and the old building is once again in use as a hall.

In 1847 the site was secured for the Catholic church in Fairview. The Church of the Visitation, built in 1855, replaced an earlier parochial chapel. The church was extended in the early years of the Twentieth Century.

ST. ANTHONY'S CHURCH, CLONTARF.

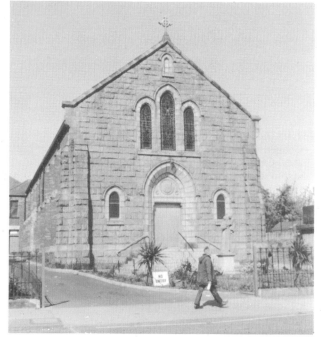

CHURCH OF THE IMMACULATE HEART OF MARY, CITY QUAY.

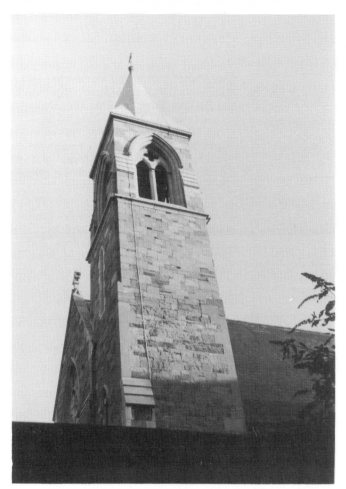

The Church of the Immaculate Heart of Mary, City Quay, was opened and blessed in 1863. The gate, railings and bell tower were added in 1887-1900. City Quay was designated a parish in 1908.

From 1913 Guinness had been loading and unloading their ships at Custom House Quay and City Quay but with the building of the Matt Talbot Memorial Bridge in 1978 it was necessary to transfer this activity further down the Liffey.

CUSTOM HOUSE AND GUINNESS BOAT, CITY QUAY.

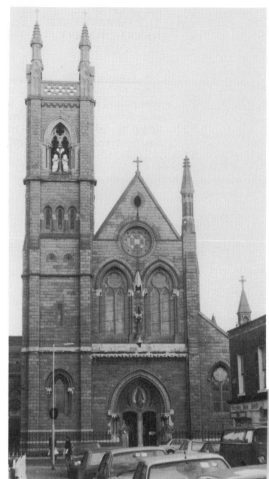

CHURCH OF ST. JOSEPH, BERKELEY STREET.

To meet the spiritual needs of the growing number of people who were moving into new houses in the area, a wooden chapel was built in Berkeley Street in 1870. The granite-faced Church of St. Joseph, designed by O'Neill and Byrne, architects, was opened in 1880. Berkeley Street Parish was constituted from St. Michan's in 1890. Mosaic and other decorative work in the church was completed before the close of the Century.

The parish served by St. Joseph's Church is commonly known as Berkeley Road although the church itself is in Berkeley Street, which connects Berkeley Road and Blessington Street.

St. Lawrence's Church of Ireland, Chapelizod, was built in 1832.

CHURCH OF THE NATIVITY OF THE BLESSED VIRGIN MARY, CHAPELIZOD.

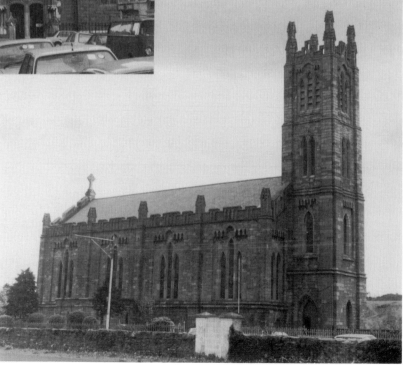

TOWER,
ST. MARY'S CHURCH,
HADDINGTON ROAD.

The tower of St. Mary's Church, Haddington Road, was designed by W. G. Doolin, who also designed St. Anthony's Church, Merchants' Quay. The foundation stone of St. Mary's Church was laid in 1837 but it was not completed until the end of the century. J. J. O'Callaghan, architect, was responsible for the design of the facade, belfry and aisles, and for the fitting of the stained glass windows.

The Boys' School, Haddington Road, designed by J. J. McCarthy, was built in the 1870s and later extended.

The apse and altar were designed by C. Geoghegan, architect, in 1879.

The parochial houses in St. Mary's Road were built in 1889 about twelve years after the road was first opened.

REAR VIEW,
ST. MARY'S CHURCH,
HADDINGTON ROAD.

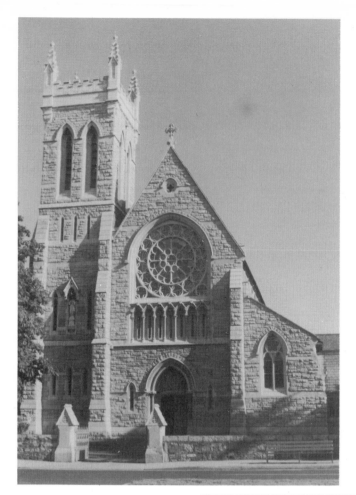

CHURCH OF THE SACRED HEART, DONNYBROOK.

The Church of the Sacred Heart, Donnybrook, was dedicated in 1866. Patrick Byrne had been appointed architect but he died before he could design the building. Pugin and Ashlin were appointed in his place. The stained glass windows of Saints Patrick, Eithne and Feidhlim are by Michael Healy. It was originally intended that the church would have a spire but it was never built.

The Sisters of Charity moved into Donnybrook Castle in 1837 and established St. Mary Magdalen's Asylum in a complex of buildings, including a laundry erected around the original castle.

St. Mary's House of Studies was established by the Discalced Carmelites at Morehampton Road in 1887 and St. Damian's Poor Clare Convent was established in Simmonscourt Road in 1906.

Dalkey Parish Church of Ireland, above Bullough Harbour, is built on the perimeter of a former granite quarry.

William Hutchinson, who was appointed Harbour Master of Dún Laoghaire in 1823, lived in Beaulah, opposite the Dalkey Parish Church.

The Church of the Assumption, Dalkey, was built in 1840.

CHURCH,
DALKEY.

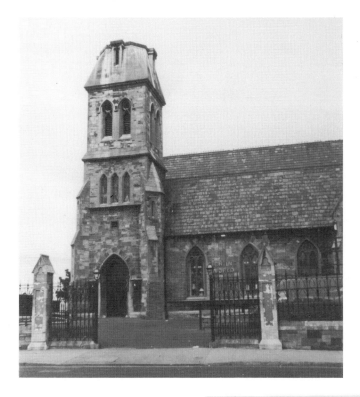

FORMER ST. JAMES'S CHURCH (C. of I.), JAMES STREET.

The former St. James's Church, designed for the Church of Ireland by Joseph Welland, architect, was built in 1861. The spire was taken down in 1949 and the building is now used as a showroom for electric light fittings.

The Gothic facade of St. Michan's Catholic Church, Halston Street, designed by G. C. Ashlin, was erected in 1893.

In 1819 Mother Mary Aikenhead and her Sisters of Charity from the original foundation in North William Street took in charge the Refuge in Stanhope Street which had been set up in the old Manor House of Grangegorman. They established a convent, laundry, industrial school and training school and provided all the necessary buildings.

St. Paul's Church was built for the Church of Ireland in 1821-24. It features a Gothic tower over the sanctuary. The building is now an enterprise centre.

FORMER ST. PAUL'S CHURCH OF IRELAND, NORTH KING STREET.

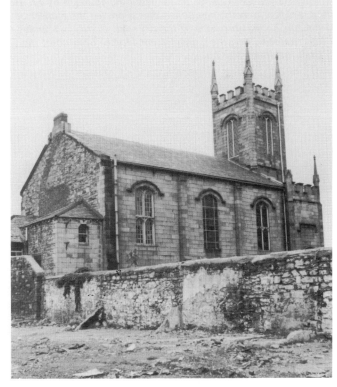

The Chapel at All Hallows' College, Drumcondra, was designed by George A. C. Ashlin and the College was designed by J. J. O'Callaghan.

The seminary was founded by the Vincentian Fathers in 1842. The building to the left of the Chapel, Drumcondra House, designed by Edward Lovett Pearce, was built for Sir Marmaduke Coghill in 1725. It was extended later and forms part of the College complex.

The Foreign Missionary College of All Hallows, founded by Fr. Hand, C.M., opened in 1842. The historian, Fr. N. Donnelly, mentioned that it proved the pioneer of several religious and educational establishments on the north side of the city – St. Patrick's Training College; the Male Blind Asylum; High Park Reformatory; the Convalescent Home, Beaumont; the Christian Brothers' Novitiate and the O'Brien Institute, Marino.

ALL
HALLOWS'
COLLEGE,
DRUMCONDRA.

CHURCH OF ST. PAUL OF THE CROSS, MOUNT ARGUS, HAROLD'S CROSS.

The site of the church and the Passionist monastery at Mount Argus was acquired in 1856. The foundation of the monastery on the banks of the Poddle was laid in 1859 and it was opened in 1863. The Romanesque church, dedicated to St. Patrick and St. Paul of the Cross, was designed by J. J. McCarthy and built in 1878. It has been altered and enlarged in the present century. An elaborate scene is depicted in the tympanum and on the pediment stands a golden statue of St. Michael the Archangel.

CHURCH AND MONASTERY, ST. PAUL'S RETREAT, MOUNT ARGUS.

DOMINICAN
PRIORY,
DOMINICK
STREET.

The first stone of the Dominican Priory, Dominick Street, was laid in 1885. The building, which adjoins the church in Dominick Street, has been altered and extended. The adjoining church, built in 1880, was designed by George A. Ashlin.

The extensive Dominican Priory in Tallaght adjoins St. Mary's Church, a photograph of which appears on the opposite page 233.

DOMINICAN
PRIORY,
TALLAGHT.

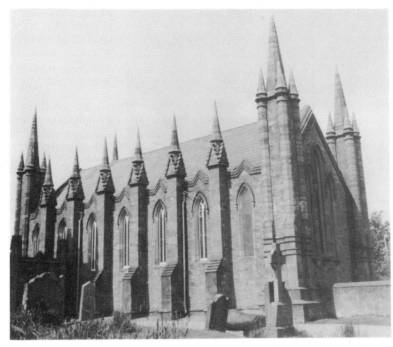

ST. MAELRUAN'S
CHURCH OF
IRELAND,
TALLAGHT.

St. Maelruan's
(Church of Ireland),
Tallaght, was built
in 1829 on the site
of an earlier church.
The adjacent Nor-
man Tower was at
one time used as an
entrance to the
church and it serves
as a bell tower.

The Order of Preachers came to Tallaght in 1842 and the Fr. Tom Burke Memorial Church, attached to St. Mary's Dominican Priory, was designed by George A. Ashlin as a conventual church and built in 1880. It now forms the transepts of the enlarged parish church built in 1970.

Other churches designed by George A. Ashlin include St. Kevin's, Harrington Street and the Church of the Annunciation, Rathfarnham.

ST. MARY'S
PARISH
CHURCH,
TALLAGHT.

PRESENTATION CONVENT, CLONDALKIN.

The convent was enlarged and other improvements carried out in 1869. The cemetery was consecrated in 1880.

The Presentation Convent in Clondalkin was founded in 1857. It followed the founding of convents by the same order in George's Hill (1794), Terenure (1807) and Maynooth (1823). Sisters from the Clondalkin convent were responsible for setting up the Lucan convent in 1867 and another convent was set up in Warrenmount in 1892. The Clondalkin convent and adjoining church were designed by F. W. Caldbeck in the Early Gothic Style. There is an octagonal belfry and spire at the eastern end and a group of four stained glass windows above the high altar.

An ornamental entrance archway and iron gates to the church, convent and schools was erected in 1891.

The belfry was raised in 1871.

CHURCH AND CONVENT, CLONDALKIN.

CHURCH OF THE NATIVITY OF THE BLESSED VIRGIN MARY, SAGGART.

The parish of Saggart is dedicated to St. Molaise who established a monastery in the area in the Seventh Century. The present Church of the Nativity of the Blessed Virgin Mary was solemnly dedicated in 1849. Main walls and central tower are constructed of coarse limestone rubble. Stone was donated by local people and transported to the site by voluntary labour. In the dignified interior there are slender cluster-shafted columns of painted timber and an imitation vaulted ceiling. The stained glass window behind the High Altar is in memory of Father John Dunne.

A Catholic church was built in Newcastle in 1813.

CHURCH, SAGGART.

ST. MARY OF THE ANGELS, CHURCH STREET.

The foundation stone of the Church of St. Mary of the Angels, designed by G. C. Ashlin, was laid by Cardinal Cullen.

The church was built in 1864.

The Capuchins also built the Father Mathew Hall, adjacent to the church.

The Church of the Assumption, Howth, was designed by W. H. Byrne and built in 1899 on a commanding site provided by Lord Howth. The granite-faced building is in the Romanesque style.

The iron-framed timber Church of St. Fintan, Sutton, has been replaced by a permanent church building.

CHURCH OF THE ASSUMPTION, HOWTH.

236

ST. TERESA'S CHURCH, CLARENDON STREET.

The Discalced Carmelite Church of St. Teresa, Clarendon Street, designed by O'Neill and Byrne, was built in the last decade of the Eighteenth Century, altered and extended in the Nineteenth Century. It has some good examples of stained glass and a fine sculpture of the Dead Christ by John Hogan.

The Holy Faith Convent, which occupied the site of the present Westbury Hotel, dated from the 1870s.

Over the years a number of different architects have been responsible for the work carried out in St. Teresa's Church, Clarendon Street.

The Calced Carmelites opened the Church of Our Lady of Mount Carmel, designed by George Papworth, in Whitefriar Street in 1827. It has been altered and extended and the main entrance is now from Aungier Steet.

In the church since 1927 is the Gothic style oak statue of Our Lady of Dublin which possibly dates back to the Fifteenth Century

CHURCH OF OUR LADY OF MOUNT CARMEL.

ST. MARY'S
PRO-CATHEDRAL,
MARLBORO STREET.

Tyrone House, on the opposite side of the road, was designed by Richard Cassels and built for the Marquis of Beresford, Earl of Tyrone. The building was acquired by the Commissioners of National Education. It is now the headquarters of the Department of Education.

St. Mary's Pro-Cathedral was designed perhaps by John Sweetman of Raheny. The foundation stone was laid in 1815 on the site previously occupied by Lord Annesley's house and the building was opened in 1825. The southern portico was added in 1837 and the front portico in 1843.

The church stands on a podium or a high platform with fluted Doric columns to the front and side which are Greek in style whereas the interior is Roman. The dome was not part of the original design.

The Anglican Free Church of the Parish of St. George and St. Thomas, Great Charles Street, was consecrated in 1828. Originally a Methodist Church, it was purchased from the Methodists by the Church of Ireland after the landlord refused to sanction its sale for use as a Catholic Church. The symmetrical granite facade is topped by a plain pediment.

THE FORMER
METHODIST CHURCH,
NOW THE ANGLICAN
CHURCH OF ST. GEORGE
AND ST. THOMAS,
GREAT CHARLES STREET.

TOWN HALL,   Foundations
BLACKROCK.   laid in 1865.

The Church of St. John the Baptist, designed by Patrick Byrne, was commenced in 1842 on a site presented by Lord Cloncury. The Church was dedicated in 1845 and additions were built in 1850 and 1856. Inside the lofty interior can be seen stained glass art by Harry Clarke and Evie Hone as well as work from the Early Studio. There are some Twentieth-Century additions to the original building.

The Congregation of the Holy Ghost moved into Blackrock in 1860 and subsequently built their College, which was extended many times.

CHURCH OF
ST. JOHN
THE BAPTIST,
BLACKROCK.

FORMER SYNAGOGUE, SOUTH CIRCULAR ROAD.

The Synagogue was built about 1925.

The Dublin Hebrew Congregation Synagogue is now in Adelaide Road.

The former granite walled church on the opposite side of the road is now in use as a mosque.

This building, on the South Circular Road, which belonged to the Dublin Hebrew Congregation, is no longer in use for its original purpose.

The synagogue, Walworth Road, opened in 1917, is now a Jewish Museum.

The small church sited on a corner in Lucan village shows simple and original use of the Gothic-style facade.

The facade of the Nineteenth Century Courthouse in Lucan has been preserved as part of the reconstructed Garda Station.

The Methodist Church, Lucan, is now used for both religious and social purposes.

METHODIST CHURCH, LUCAN.

ST. SAVIOUR'S CHURCH, DOMINICK STREET.

The foundation stone of St. Saviour's Church, Dominick Street, was laid in 1852 and the building, designed by J. J. McCarthy, was dedicated in 1861.

The first stone of the Dominican priory designed by J. L. Robinson, was laid in 1885. The building, which adjoins the church in Dominick Street, has been altered and extended.

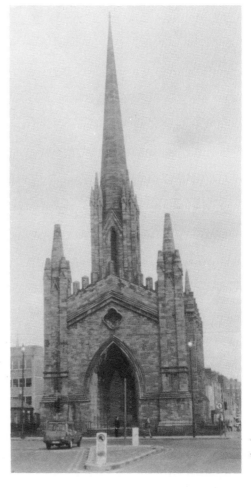

St. Mary's Chapel of Ease to the Church of Ireland now used for secular purposes, was designed by John Semple and completed in 1839. Popularly known as "The Black Church", on account of its walls of Dublin calp stone, it has a parabolic vaulted interior, galleries, lancet windows and a slender spire.

Other churches designed by John Semple include those in Rathmines, Donnybrook, Tallaght, Whitechurch, Kilternan and Monkstown.

ST. MARY'S CHAPEL-OF-EASE, "THE BLACK CHURCH", ST. MARY'S PLACE.

GARRISON CHURCH OF THE SACRED HEART, ARBOUR HILL.

The Garrison Church, Arbour Hill, built in 1848 was consecrated for use as a Catholic Church in 1927.

Arbour Hill Military Hospital and Prison date back to 1797. The Royal Military Infirmary was superseded in 1910 by the Hospital at Arbour Hill. This hospital is now known as St. Brican's. The Detention Barracks, now a civilian prison, was opened in 1848. Pádraic Pearse was imprisoned here. He and other 1916 leaders shot in Kilmainham Jail were buried in the cemetery behind the church.

In 1922 the prison at Arbour Hill was taken over by the Irish Army. Mountjoy Prison, designed by Joshua Jebb, was built in the 1880s and enlarged later.

PRISON
HOSPITAL,
ARBOUR HILL.

ROUND TOWER, PROSPECT CEMETERY, GLASNEVIN.

Prospect Cemetery, Glasnevin, was founded in 1831 and in later years it was greatly extended to meet the growing need for burial space near the city. The original boundary walls incorporate watch towers.

Daniel O'Connell was the founder of Prospect Cemetery and the round tower, designed by George Petrie, was erected over his vault.

Mount Jerome Cemetery was laid out in 1835 and the adjacent Church of Ireland was built in 1847.

The Cemetery at Dean's Grange, was opened in 1865.

The Mortuary Chapel in Prospect Cemetery, Glasnevin, was built in 1878. The design is based on Cormac's Chapel, Cashel.

The mortuary chapel, lodge and railings were designed by J. J. McCarthy and date from about 1878.

MORTUARY CHAPEL, PROSPECT CEMETERY, GLASNEVIN.

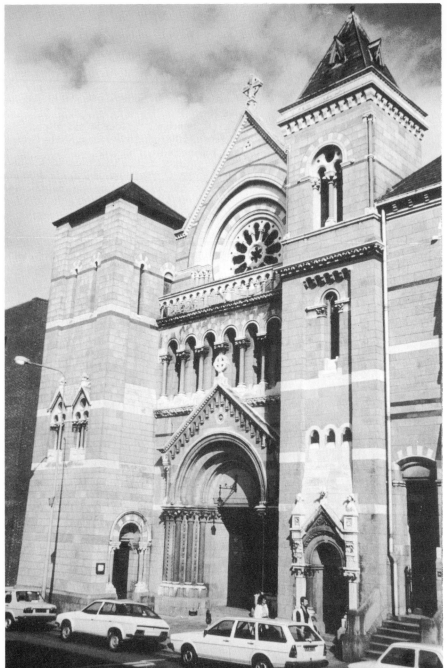

St. Ann's parish was formed in 1707 and the original basilican style church, designed by Isaac Wills, was commenced about 1720. Extensive alterations and improvements were carried out about 1860 but the facade, as originally designed, was never completed. The present polychromatic Romanesque style facade, designed by Deane and Woodward, was built in 1868 in front of the earlier one but the twin towers which the architects had envisaged never materialised. There are stained glass windows by the Irish born artist Wilhelmena Geddes and the reredos is finished in Venetian mosaic.

INDEX TO BUILDINGS ILLUSTRATED

DUBLIN'S ARCHITECTURAL DEVELOPMENT
1800-1925

by

MATTHEW J. McDERMOTT
B.Arch., F.R.I.A.I.

Edited and Illustrated by

AODHAGÁN BRIOSCÚ
B. Arch.

Published
by
TULCAMAC
Dublin
Distributed by Well Red, 6 Crowe Street,
Dublin 2.
Telephone 01–771507

DUBLIN'S ARCHITECTURAL DEVELOPMENT 1800-1925

First published March 1988.   All rights reserved.

Main text (eight chapters) © Copyright Matthew J. McDermott.

Photographs and Commentary © Copyright Aodhagán Brioscú.

INTERNATIONAL STANDARD BOOK NUMBERS
ISBN Paperback Edition   1 871212 01 4
ISBN Hardback Edition   1 871212 00 6

The cover is based on the drawing by T. Raffles Brown of Sir Thomas Manly Deane's design for the National Library and the National Museum, Kildare Street.

The drawing, which also shows Leinster House, Merrion Square, Dublin Bay and Howth, is reproduced with the kind co-operation and permission of the National Museum.

The book design, layout and editing are by Aodhagán Brioscú.

TULCAMAC, GEALÁRAS, AN BRIOTÁS, CONTAE ÁTHA CLIATH. FÓN 01–582121.